MANAGING PRIORITIES

HOW TO CREATE BETTER PLANS AND MAKE SMARTER DECISIONS

T0289726

BY

HARRY MAX

FOREWORD BY LUKE HOHMANN

TWO WAVES

BOOKS

TWO WAVES BOOKS

NEW YORK, NY, USA

"Prioritization is one of the most challenging things we do in our personal and professional lives on a daily basis. We implicitly prioritize without truly understanding how, often leaving us with a lack of clarity on how to make trade-off decisions and leading us to avoid the most important tasks. In *Managing Priorities*, Harry Max provides practical frameworks to show us how to set priorities with intention in a relatable, useful, and entertaining read."

—Wendy Shepperd, SVP Engineering, SailPoint

"People have long known it is important to have clear priorities and then focus on them. But no one ever tells you how to do it. But that's exactly what Harry Max does in *Managing Priorities*, where he clearly lays out the steps that anyone can use to be more productive and effective. It's required reading for anyone wanting to be a better business leader."

—Marc Randolph, co-founder and first CEO of Netflix

"The difference between a life of reacting and a life of purpose comes down to priorities. In this excellent book, Harry Max clearly describes the key elements of prioritization, how it works, and how you can put it to work for yourself, your team, and your organization. Harry Max is one of the smartest people I know. So, I would read any book he chose to write. And lucky for me, lucky for all of us, he chose to write a book about choosing how to choose. Thanks, Harry!"

—Dave Gray, founder, School of the Possible, and co-author of
Gamestorming: A Playbook for Innovators, Rulebreakers, and Changemakers

"*Managing Priorities* by Harry Max is a compelling guide for managers and leaders who find themselves navigating the interconnected complexities of modern business. Max's exploration into prioritization offers readers valuable insights and skills for applying prioritization across all aspects of professional life and provides practical strategies to apply in their own organizations. This book is a must-read for anyone who wants to create a culture of clarity and purpose in their organization, from small teams to large enterprises."

—Mark Interrante, former SVP Engineering at Dell and Salesforce

"Harry has taken a topic that is important to all business leaders, prioritizing. He has written the most comprehensive book that has ever been written on the topic of prioritizing."

—Eric Lofholm, CEO, Being Movement International

"Not enough people understand the need for prioritization. This book provides an extremely tactical toolkit to address the challenge of prioritization both on a personal and professional level, providing the frameworks that enable a solid foundation for action. This is a great resource that you will find yourself referencing on a regular basis."

—Colleene Isaacs, entrepreneur

"*Managing Priorities* employs a brilliantly simple approach to demystify the 'how' of prioritizing, ultimately paving the way for improved decisions and outcomes."

—Bob Cagle, co-founder/CEO productOps, Inc.

"After reading *Managing Priorities: How to Create Better Plans and Make Smarter Decisions*, it became apparent to me that this book should be a mandatory part of all business curricula. The DEGAP strategy is applicable to all levels of management, from small businesses to corporate entities, in establishing their priorities. Priorities can teach managers, directors, supervisors, and CEOs valuable lessons on communicating effectively and properly delegating tasks to employees."

—Franchette Dyer, CEO of Vetech Business Services, LLC

"Every time I put Harry's methods into practice, my teams level up and so do I. Now you can too."

—Jess McMullin, founder, Objective Lenses

"Prioritization is a team sport. Harry's DEGAP process is immediately useful. A must-read. Prioritize *Managing Priorities!*"

—Scott Sehlhorst, President of Tyner Blain, Product Management and Strategy Consultant

"*Managing Priorities* provides a front-row seat to easily learn and apply Harry's practical and systematic roadmap to achieve major results. Full of brilliant, easy-to-use nuggets, his system enables success in any endeavor."

—Ward Ashman, Ph.D., founder and inventor, Trimergence

"Prioritization either seems like something that just takes care of itself or is a simple enough matter of following a process. Harry Max has something far deeper and more rigorous to offer. Tools, yes, but, equally if not more important, also a path into a powerful way of thinking about how to decide what matters."

—Michael Anton Dila, complexity thinker, originator of System 3

"To live a fulfilling life with purpose in both our personal and professional lives, we need to understand the artful execution of prioritizing our priorities. Emphasizing the human aspect of prioritization, Max's book offers an easy-to-follow process and diverse frameworks for any situation."

—Ashley Blake, President of Ash & Co. Consulting

"This book is for anyone who has needed to figure out how to get things done, so…everyone. Max goes through, step by step, with vivid stories and examples, how to find the best path to accomplish your goals. Better yet, he also catalogs all the ways to solve this problem making this an indispensable guide to how, when and who decides what to get done."

—Maryann Kongovi, operations executive

Managing Priorities
How to Create Better Plans and Make Smarter Decisions

By Harry Max

Two Waves Books,
an imprint of Rosenfeld Media
125 Maiden Lane
New York, New York 10038
USA

On the Web: www.rosenfeldmedia.com
Please send errata to: errata@rosenfeldmedia.com

Publisher: Louis Rosenfeld
Managing Editor: Marta Justak
Illustrations: Mark Hill
Developmental Editor: Adam Rosen
Interior Layout: Danielle Foster
Cover Design: Heads of State
Illustrators: Mark Hill and Danielle Foster
Indexer: Marilyn Augst
Proofreader: Sue Boshers

To my mom and family of birth,
as well as my family of choice.

Special thanks to
Rosanne Cash

Contents and Executive Summary

Part 3. Putting Process into Practice   67

Apply DEGAP to individuals, teams, and organizations.

Foreword

"I should be doing something else instead of writing this foreword," I thought as I sat down at my laptop. Like you, I have a bunch of items on my personal and professional to-do lists. And like you, all of them are "more important" than writing this foreword or reading this book.

And yet...here we found ourselves. Me, writing a foreword to a much-needed, wonderful book. You, reading it, hoping that this book will help you be more successful (it should). Or at least a bit less neurotic (it will).

Prioritization is as much about accepting the complexities of our personal and professional lives as it is about making choices in navigating that complexity so that we can make, as the book promises, smarter decisions that help us progress against, accomplish, and even celebrate victory as we cross items off our to-do lists, celebrate the release of a new product, acquire a degree, start or sell a company, or like Harry, publish a book about prioritization.

A book that helps us understand the complexities of prioritization. A book that helps us understand the mindset we need to create priorities that align with our values and help us achieve our goals. A book that guides us in understanding how teams, and teams of teams, can prioritize their work to create individual and shared success.

Now that this book is in your hands, prioritize reading it. Prioritize putting its advice into practice. Buy copies for everyone you care about and work with, and keep it handy on your bookshelf because, as Harry outlines, prioritization done well has a natural cadence that contributes to our individual and collective sense of well-being.

And if you find yourself torn by the decision to prioritize writing a foreword for a friend's book over doing some other work, relax.

You prioritized the right activity for the right reasons.

—Luke Hohmann, husband, father, author, entrepreneur
Chief Innovation Officer, Applied Frameworks and SAFe® Fellow

1

Why Prioritize?

If you want to know what's actually important to you, take a look at how you spend your days. Change your priorities, change your future.

—Seth Godin

1

The Missing Ingredient

I t was autumn of 2014 in the Northwest, and the first time I'd been to Tacoma, Washington. This wasn't an obvious hotel for a corporate workshop—not boutique-y at all—more like the "ranch-style, you-could-be-anywhere" type. The breakfast room had community tables draped with synthetic white tablecloths, so writing a to-do list on them with my Space Pen was out of the question.

Staring back at me through the glass sneeze guard were scrambled eggs, floppy bacon, oily sausages, and partially cooked hash browns. I set the halves of my bagel on the toaster conveyor belt, round-side down. Another day, another hotel breakfast.

I was hopeful that the 21st Century Leadership workshop I was here to attend would be a good change of pace. I'd been sent to Tacoma by Rackspace, the San Antonio–based cloud-computing company where I'd been working as VP of Product & Experience Design for several years. The senior leadership team (SLT) had suggested that this conference, and perhaps some time away from corporate headquarters, could do me some good.

By this point, Rackspace had outgrown its scrappy startup origins, but it was still a far cry from the behemoth it is today as I write these words: a company that posts over $3 billion in annual revenue and has over 6,500 employees working in over a dozen locations around the globe.

My mind wandered back four years prior to this conference, to when I was lured to Texas from California, the only place I'd lived and worked since high school, by my friend and former colleague, Mark, who would soon turn out to be my boss.

"Take a long weekend," Mark had insisted as we sat upstairs at Red Rock Coffee in Mountain View in 2010, about a mile from Google headquarters. "Check out the Castle. Meet Lanham, the CEO, and Lew, the president. See for yourself. It'll be fun."

"The Castle?" I scratched my head. "Let me think about it."

Two weeks later, Mark picked me up at the San Antonio airport. We got off 35, made a right, and drove up to a massive building surrounded by a sea of blacktop. Mark explained that Rackspace was housed in a converted shopping mall, but I had imagined it was a lot smaller. Outside the main entrance, there was a galvanized water tower brandishing the words "Home of Fanatical Support." Intriguing.

Even with Mark's earlier download, I was quite unprepared for what was to come when he flashed his badge and the receptionist waved us in. I stepped out of the cool San Antonio air and into the bustle of a corporate amusement park: various flags hung from the 25-foot ceiling as phones rang, computers whirred, and people hustled this way and that. A spiral slide connected the second floor to the ground floor. The people in front of me looked to be hard at work, and yet their smiles and laughter and sense of spirited collaboration made it clear that everybody was having a hell of a lot of fun.

"Inconceivable!" I thought to myself, channeling my inner Vizzini from *The Princess Bride* (as one does). I knew right then and there I'd be moving to Texas. That is, if they'd have me.

A vibration in my pocket jolted me back to Tacoma. It was Gigi, Rackspace's VP of Engineering.

"Everything okay?" I asked.

"Not really. Mark is out," she said, her voice uncharacteristically shaky.

"What do you mean he's 'out'?"

"They announced it this morning. They replaced *our* Mark. Can you friggin' believe it?"

She interrupted me before I had time to fumble out a response. "Can you come back? We need you here. Now."

"Sh*t," I said, not entirely under my breath. My heart sank.

I probably should have seen this coming. Six months earlier, when Lew (the president and Mark's boss) stepped down, I wondered how long the Rackspace ride would last. Then, a few short months after that, our beloved CEO, Lanham, the living embodiment of Rackspace culture, was unceremoniously ousted by the Board of Directors.[1] It stunk, but leadership changes like this happen sometimes when an organization changes strategic direction or top priorities.

One half of my bagel slid off the conveyer belt in all its mostly toasted glory, taking me back to the matter at hand. "What good will it do?" I asked.

A newfound clarity presented itself in Gigi's voice. "I don't know exactly. You keep everybody calm."

It was an interesting observation, if not a touch ironic. Funny how consuming copious amounts of espresso can help one keep other people calm. "Let me see when I can get a flight."

In those four minutes, I experienced what Elon Musk, love him or hate him, euphemistically refers to as an "unplanned disassembly."[2] Now all our best-laid plans, the decisions they were based on, and the priorities we had

---

1. Lanham Napier and Becca Braun, *Billion or Bust: Growing a Tech Company in Texas*, read by Nathan Agin (Braun Collection, 2023), Audible audiobook, unabr., 4 hrs.
2. "Rapid Unplanned Disassembly," *The Economist*, July 2, 2015, www.economist.com/science-and-technology/2015/07/02/rapid-unplanned-disassembly

stacked on top of one another were all up in the air, spinning wildly like those numbered balls in a novelty bingo machine.

What should we do next? What *could* we do? How could I help to right the ship? Was it even *possible* to right it? If Mark couldn't make it work, how could I, someone not on the SLT, possibly help?

Figuring all of this out was going to take a lot more than a one-person crisis response in a hotel breakfast room. It was going to take a systematic approach, a rigorous process that would make it crystal clear what mattered and what didn't. It was all about priorities. Fortunately for me, everything I had accomplished up to this point in my career—on purpose and sometimes not—revolved around developing such a system.

I hung up and called the office, informing them that, God willing, I was going to be back at the Castle by the end of the day. I had a job to do.

● ● ●

For companies and organizations to survive, they need to prioritize. But to thrive, their priorities must mesh like gears to synchronize the work that teams are planning and doing, so they can make progress consistently and predictably. And those teams, in turn, must be composed of individual contributors and front-line managers who are tightly aligned, laser focused, and exceptionally productive.

None of these statements are controversial; chances are you agree with them yourself. However, as soon as you step into the real world, you see how much easier it is to make these pronouncements than to implement them. In too many companies (perhaps yours?), workers are overwhelmed, stressed out, and have a vague sense they are not working on the right things or making enough progress. Teams seem to be working at cross-purposes and juggling too many priority ones (an irony worth thinking about).

The results are sadly predictable. Supposedly, must-do, no-fail organizational goals don't get started, completed, or resourced adequately. Executives' pet projects suck up precious resources. And morale—to say nothing of revenue—is well below what it could be. And all throughout the organization, there's a nagging sense that things could be better. *A lot better.*

In hindsight, many of these tragic organizational failures are painfully obvious and often perfectly preventable. But what to do? Who has the luxury of hindsight or a huge interest in waiting around until things implode before doing what you can to chart a better course?

How Did We Get Here?

On the surface, there may appear to be many different reasons a company finds itself in utter misalignment. But, in my experience, almost all organizational troubles originate from a single cause: senior executives or administrators and frontline personnel seem to be living in alternate dimensions. Leadership is primarily concerned with figuring out what to do and why. Frontline management and personnel focus on how to pull it off and when.

This dissonance has steep costs: declining performance, eroding market share, crumbling brand reputation, and dwindling value for customers, shareholders, and other critical stakeholders. But the hidden costs may be even more insidious.

Doubling down on the wrong priorities is all but guaranteed to create an endless stream of burnt-out and overwhelmed individuals, no one more so than the new or newly promoted manager. The newly minted manager's passion and commitment to quality—the very talents that got them noticed in the first place—quickly become casualties of excessive competing interests. Before long, constant demands disconnected from explicit strategy and direction, coupled with an underlying drumbeat to do even more, faster, now, reduce them to an exhausted, reactive shell just looking to get through the day.

Having the right priorities, and the self-discipline to limit those priorities, can offer a way out of this mess. Prioritization is the process of identifying items of any type and arranging them in order of importance, superiority in rank, or privilege. It's the antidote to accelerating fragmentation, a defense against the infinite distractions that keep individuals, teams, and organizations from operating at peak potential. It's the missing ingredient in a recipe that's not quite right. Prioritization was, as you will discover over the course of this book, what helped me contribute to stabilizing the situation at Rackspace and turning things around at other companies since then.

Often when people hear the term *prioritization*, their mind points to personal productivity gurus and time management hacks. They think of tasks, to-do lists, and other techniques for getting more out of their day. These tips certainly have their place, but they aren't the focus of this book. My main focus here is on deciding *what* to consider rather than concrete strategies for getting things done during your workweek (though we will touch on this some).

Prioritization is a lot harder than it might sound. For one, finding good resources on the topic is a challenge. Actionable, how-to information is too often buried deep in the guts of books, blogs, videos, and the like. And when useful information on prioritization is available, it's usually not identified as such, which makes it hard to find.

In addition, in much of the business world, prioritization is typically the purview of project management, product development, and annual planning. The outcome is that management tends to view prioritization as no more than choosing which projects get funded or which products, services, features, and widgets should be built. In this view, prioritization isn't a process—it's a light switch.

Although they may not realize it, many organizations *do* have access to proven approaches for defining high-quality priorities. There are companies and consultants that specialize in it and powerful methodologies and tools available if you know where to look.

But in this regard, companies are like people: they don't know what they don't know. They simply rely on what they've done previously, reusing improvised approaches that spit out unrefined "priorities." The problem isn't just that they are prioritizing poorly, but that they aren't even aware it's the keystone problem to everything else, so they *don't* and *can't* fix it.

These slapdash priorities, in turn, become the inputs to their financial and operational planning processes. The results, again, are predictable: the lack of rigor and clearly defined objectives invariably leads to resource conflicts that ripple across the organization over time. Perhaps there's a better way.

My approach, honed over my thirty years in the trenches of Silicon Valley and articulated in this book, is to make the process of prioritizing a first-class citizen. I offer a repeatable process and simple taxonomy for prioritizing anything, as well as including strategies, tactics, techniques, and tools you can use depending on your individual needs. I separate episodic, one-off efforts from periodic and continuous prioritization. Lastly, I look at the important differences between prioritizing for yourself and setting group priorities as a member of a team or a larger organization.

Proper prioritization grants a deep competitive advantage to the people, teams, and companies that master it. Yet, if you're like most people, you don't have a great model for doing it. I'm here to help.

Who Is This Book For?

I like to think of this book as a short self-help course for businesses.

Managing Priorities: How to Create Better Plans and Make Smarter Decisions combines real stories, practical tools, and timeless insights to equip anyone interested in becoming a more effective manager or leader with the skills, knowledge, and mindset to prioritize anything, anytime, anywhere. Being able to identify what true priorities are and are not, understanding the process of prioritizing, and learning to recognize the inputs and outputs of successful prioritization are all deeply valuable skills. Use this book to create more impactful plans and make better informed decisions. Use it to do a better job. Use it to lower your stress.

More specifically, though, this book is geared toward new or recently promoted managers and entrepreneurs involved in strategy activation, planning, or resource allocation in companies or organizations, for-profit or not. It's for people who have recently increased, or want to increase, their scope of responsibility and are not yet overly committed to the status quo and default approaches. It's also for students of business looking for a helpful primer on management.

The overarching theme of this book is business, regardless of industry. It does not offer domain-specific solutions, methodologies, or protocols for fields such as clinical healthcare, education, emergency response, or the military. Moreover, this book assumes a certain degree of knowledge. It is not meant for those readers seeking an introduction to managing people, projects, money, or data. What it does provide are strategies, tactics, tools, and techniques that are applicable across entire ranges of disciplines—including, most likely, yours. This book, and the processes it describes, can benefit leaders in almost every industry.

2

The Power of Priorities

If you squint long enough, you'll start to see everything at work as a prioritization problem or an opportunity. Truly great organizations have figured this out. So, they push hard to get their priorities straight. Their leadership, management, and front-line workers alike work hard at purposefully "...closing the gap between the accidental and intentional,"[1] to know what matters most and stay focused on it in the face of uncertainty and change. Because of this, they are positioned to take better advantage of good luck and are less likely to fall prey to bad luck[2] or black swans,[3] like a global pandemic.

---

1. Ken Kocienda, *Creative Selection: Inside Apple's Design Process During the Golden Age of Steve Jobs*, read by Ken Kocienda (Macmillan Audio, 2018), Audible audiobook, unabr., 7 hrs., 28 min.
2. Jim Collins and Morton T. Hansen, *Great by Choice* (New York, NY: Random House Business, October 2011), EPub ed.
3. Nassim Taleb, *The Black Swan: The Impact of the Highly Improbable* (New York, NY: Random House, 2010).

That being the case, consider the possibility that *prioritize* is the most important verb in business.[4] Identifying and arranging items in order of importance, superiority in rank, or privilege is the basis for everything you do. In some ways, you are the sum of your choices at any given moment in time. And it's up to each of you to choose which branch you are going to follow. When you are conscious of your priorities, they become the input to your plans and decisions. Priorities represent options. If they are not explicit, they influence your unconscious choices and actions. Prioritizing forms the mental software that empowers people to make tough trade-offs and execute with confidence and clarity of purpose. When priorities are on target, you are more likely to stay in control of the timeline—the invisible thread that connects possible futures to present reality through the facts of the past.

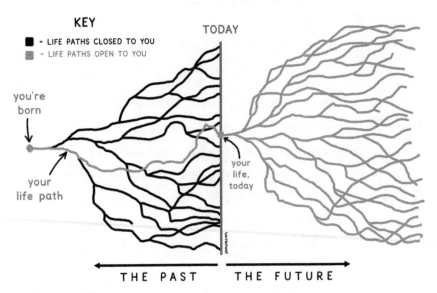

The power of priorities.

Clear priorities allow teams to act as supercharged and coordinated units, powering organizations to work with unity of purpose, more like Apple and Amazon, and less like WeWork and Webvan. "Every choice you make leads to the next choice, which leads to the next, and I know it's hard to know

4. Used with permission by Luke Hohmann.

sometimes which path to take," said Taylor Swift at NYU's 2022 commencement ceremony.

To do this day-in-and-day-out, though, you need to go meta—in other words, to prioritize *prioritization*. This means putting prioritizing before everything else to align people's voices and efforts to avoid working at cross purposes.

Prioritize prioritization.

Knowing your priorities is critical because even unconscious priorities direct your attention to what *seems* most important at any given moment, whether it truly is or is not. Being aware of your priorities helps you create better plans, make smarter decisions, and, ultimately, take more effective actions. The fact is, your priorities link your options to your choices, your choices to your decisions, your decisions to your actions, and your behavior to the outcomes that you *do* or *do not* achieve.

This all sounds pretty reasonable, right? Well, here's the rub: It doesn't take much more than turning on the news, reading your social media feeds, or taking a critical look at what's going on with your family, kids, friends, colleagues, or business partners to know that human beings are terrible at prioritizing prioritization.

The vast majority of people, teams, and organizations are swamped. They are overwhelmed and have a vague sense that they are not deploying their limited energy on the right stuff. They are failing to make progress. They don't know how to deal with the oncoming future before events have flown out of control. "They are left with the least-bad option as their best move, instead of having their best option be their best move,"[5] said Scott Sehlhorst, president of the Tyner Blain, Inc., management consultancy.

The pervasiveness of all this overload raises an obvious question: *why*? Why are you so busy, with so little time available to prioritize?

Although everyone's individual causes may vary, inevitably there's an overarching theme tying them together: a false sense of urgency.

What You Lose When Urgency Wins

In 1967, Charles Hummel, the president of Barrington College in Rhode Island, wrote a booklet titled *Tyranny of the Urgent*. What was meant as a short meditation on one of the challenges of life quickly became a bestselling text. Hummel argued that always operating in a state of "urgency" was a threat to important-but-not-urgent problems, opportunities, and tasks vying for your precious time and energy.

Hummel's thesis highlights a festering tension between short-term objectives and longer-term goals. Most of the time, unfortunately, the supposedly urgent short-term objective wins. When it does, typically what matters even more loses. It's the result of blowback from having a false sense of urgency.[6] And what's truly important often becomes urgent at the most inconvenient times.[7]

As Hummel cited, focusing on short-term results can create a nasty trap. At the individual level, it leads to feeling overworked and frustrated. No matter how hard you try, your attention and energy get swept away by the riptide of current events. The residue is the unsettling feeling (and possible reality) that you are falling further and further behind.

---

5. Used with permission by Scott Sehlhorst.
6. John P. Kotter, *A Sense of Urgency* (Boston, MA: Harvard Business Review Press, 2008).
7. Charles E. Hummel, *Tyranny of the Urgent*, rev. and expanded (Downers Grove, IL: InterVarsity Press, 2013).

Now, take this tendency of human beings to attend first to what is urgent and magnify it across multiple people and multiple teams. This situation is what happens in too many organizations where winning requires teams to work together to respond to competing requirements and constraints. Amid all the chaos, it's forgotten that coordinated actions taken now contribute to better results and desired outcomes in the future.

Coordinated action, of course, demands that people work together to come up with options and then take decisive action on them. If, as in so many cases, team members have limited information in the face of ever-expanding uncertainty, a special kind of focus is needed. Where does this focus come from? Having laser-sharp priorities is the answer.

Priorities Are Everywhere

Priorities exist in every important domain of life: business, work, family, government, education, and health (financial, physical, and mental). No matter what the context, the overarching process of prioritizing is largely the same.

However, different kinds of situations, contexts, or venues lend themselves to one of three variations based on time. *Episodic* prioritization is relegated to one-off or infrequent situations, such as when you make a large purchase or need to think through a complex decision. *Periodic* prioritization is appropriate when priorities need to be updated or refreshed at regular intervals. *Continuous* prioritization is the ongoing practice of smoothly prioritizing and reprioritizing in a mindful, Zen-like way as new information reveals itself. The distinction, especially between episodic and periodic prioritization, will become more useful in Part 3, "Putting Process into Practice," where each chapter will focus on one or the other; that is, the episodic or periodic variation.

All three types of prioritization help people refocus after distractions or interruptions knock them off track. However, both periodic and continuous prioritization (even more so) increase the number of opportunities to adjust plans or make fresh decisions before it's too late to do anything about it.

Therefore, whether you seek to improve your focus in your personal life or your concerns are purely business-related, the process of prioritizing centers on attacking the right problems and tackling the right opportunities and then enabling expedient action and progress. Its usefulness lies in the fact that it's widely applicable to almost any situation, regardless of the specific circumstances.

In a world of continuous, accelerating change and unprecedented global disruptions, the ability to navigate through the haze of uncertainty has become imperative. Better, more-adaptive approaches are needed to relieve the increasing pressure on people, teams, and organizations, all of whom need more durable ways to figure out what really matters and chart a safe course into the future.

What Prioritization Feels Like

How will you know when you've cracked the riddle of prioritization? When you realize that you are in control of the timeline, more often than not. For instance, when your boss inevitably asks you to take on yet another project, you will be able to respond more constructively and accurately, fully aware of the relative importance of their request.

When you are in control of the timeline, you can respond in a positive, confident tone. You'll be able to say "yes" to what you need to say yes to. You can say "no" or "not yet" with confidence and clarity. You will know when to focus on one thing…and when to focus on the other. This is essential when you need to foster and preserve important relationships, and it's particularly critical in highly matrixed organizations, where trust is the basis for getting stuff done.

As a budding expert in prioritization, you will be in a position to identify all the trade-offs you are facing and then successfully pick which ones you can live with. And if you find yourself needing to renegotiate existing commitments to make room for new ones, you will be on solid ground.

If all of this resonates with you, there's a good chance that you, your team, or your organization are being challenged in a way that could be markedly improved through a more intentional approach to prioritization.

The good news is this: It's not that hard to learn and do better. As the universe continues to throw new obstacles and opportunities at you, prioritizing prioritization will give you an unshakeable new foundation for creating better plans and making better decisions. It's an extreme form of upstream thinking, a powerful way to get in front of problems before they happen.

When you devote the time and space at work and in your daily life to establish clear priorities, it becomes a force multiplier. It improves your ability to deliver the right stuff. So, how do you do this? The next chapter will introduce my simple yet powerful method—*DEGAP* ®.

2

Trust the Process

Even more important than what
you think, how you think matters.

—Atul Gawande

3

Decide to Prioritize Intentionally

T he story continues. It's October 2014. The plane lurches to an abrupt stop. Pressing my nose against the window, I see faces staring back at me through the gate window at San Antonio International. The people around me start standing up, so I follow their lead and unbuckle my seatbelt. "How hard could it be?" I wonder. I know Rackspace, and I know how to prioritize. Maybe all the senior leadership changes won't be as catastrophic as I was imagining after all? Well, I would find out soon one way or another.

$$\bullet \ \bullet \ \bullet$$

It's true—prioritization isn't that complicated. But it's not simply a one-two punch of identifying items and then arranging them in order of importance either.

By *items*, I mean *potential priorities*. Items are not genuine priorities until you prioritize them.

Once you do, some will be dominant (more important), and others will be dominated (less important). Note that I use the term *items* here instead of the word *things* because *things* mean something special in the context of prioritization. *Things* is one of several categories of potential priorities. It represents inanimate objects like equipment, machinery, hardware, or tools.

To understand the process of prioritization, I find it helpful to compare it to the process of design or animation in the fields of product development and computer-generated animation, respectively. In these two disciplines, a broader process model surrounds the specific set of procedures of "designing" or "animating"—i.e., the specific, in-the-moment task of animating a character itself is distinct from all the actions that make up the larger process. Animation is a set of cascading tasks, only one of which is animating.

A process model is helpful because it provides structure and an overarching workflow that helps ensure you don't skip critical steps, some of which may bite back another day when it's time to transition from thinking to doing.

The model for prioritization involves building a metaphorical bridge for closing the gap between the "as-is" state and a more desirable future state. The bridge helps you see what your options are for getting from here to there— what you need to pay attention to and what you can safely ignore. "A good structure is something you can trust," wrote Sönke Ahrens, author of the underground bestseller *How to Take Smart Notes*.[1] Or, if you can't trust your bridge, you're on shaky ground.

The DEGAP prioritization process model has five phases:

1. **Decide** to prioritize prioritization (or not).
2. **Engage** in the process with commitment.
3. **Gather** the items to be prioritized.
4. **Arrange** the items and information you've gathered.
5. **Prioritize** using frameworks, sorting techniques, etc.

Decide, Engage, Gather, Arrange, and Prioritize—or *DEGAP* for short— is the essential process for successful prioritization when it really matters. Or, if you prefer, it's the missing ingredient. So, is DEGAP what this book is about? Or is it about how to actually navigate the prioritization of items?

---

1. Sönke Ahrens, *How to Take Smart Notes: One Simple Technique to Boost Writing, Learning and Thinking* (Self-pub., 2017).

The answer is both. The first four phases of the process model, DEG and A, set up how to generate the items, whatever they happen to be, that you then need to prioritize. The last phase, P, is where you, your team, or your organization arrange those items in order of importance.

After learning how to DEGAP, you will be well equipped to close the gap between where you are and where you want or need to be. To this end, the rest of Part 2 is devoted to dissecting each of the five phases of the DEGAP process.

• • •

You prioritize every day, either on purpose or by default. Most of us prioritize waking up on time, brushing our teeth, feeding the kids and the dog (or cat), and making a pot of coffee in the morning. You also probably prioritize having dinner or checking in at work. Even if you don't consciously consider these tasks "priorities," they are. After all, you've chosen to spend your limited time during the day doing them.

At the Decide phase, your job is to determine if it's necessary to prioritize intentionally. It's about figuring out if the upside benefits of carving out the time and going through the process of prioritizing intentionally will outweigh the downside costs of simply letting priorities emerge as reality reveals itself in the moment.

It's about responding to the prompt to *think before you act*. Will you act in an intentional and explicit way, even if that means having to pause what you're doing now, painful as that might be?

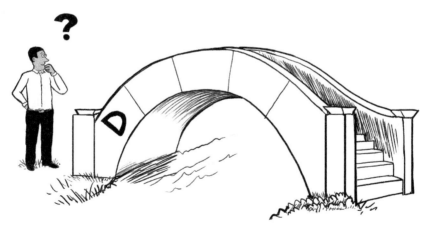

DEGAP: Decide phase.

Making the decision to engage in the process of prioritizing means that you are committing to following through with DEGAP. You are saying no to other immediate demands on your attention and saying yes to the work of engaging, gathering, arranging, and prioritizing items. You are deciding that the clarity you will gain from prioritization is more valuable than immediately attacking your endless list of to-dos, projects, and other obligations.

The first and perhaps most important part of deciding involves determining whether you have enough time to run through the remaining steps of the process. Turns out that there are plenty of situations in which, given a moment to reflect, you'll realize that you do, in fact, have enough time to slow down and prioritize prioritization. But it would be foolish to say this is always the case. However, sometimes there are moments you won't have enough time to plan because stuff is flying at you too quickly to do anything other than duck. The focus of *Managing Priorities: How to Create Better Plans and Make Smarter Decisions* is on the former—being more methodical—and, therefore, learning how to reduce the frequency of the latter.

Now, if you're unsure whether you can afford the time to prioritize intentionally, you can use a simple but powerful framework called the *Eisenhower Matrix*, or test your situation against the five most common circumstances outlined in the "Situation Checklist" section to help you decide. Both provide clarity when it's not obvious what to do next.

The Eisenhower Matrix

Popularized by Stephen Covey in his 1989 business and self-help bestseller *The 7 Habits of Highly Effective People*, the Eisenhower Matrix is arguably the best general-purpose tool for helping you figure out whether something needs your attention now or can tolerate a delay in attention or action. Its power is in its simplicity. But it falls short in situations where more sophisticated approaches are required.

President Dwight D. Eisenhower's deceptively simple technique lets you quickly triage items, especially when there's almost no time to think before you act. Plus, it gives you a set of easy-to-remember buckets where you can park items that you aren't ready to deal with in the heat of the moment.

You can use the Eisenhower Matrix to determine quickly if it's appropriate to run the DEGAP process or shelve it for the time being. Here's how it works.

	Not Urgent	Urgent
Important	NEXT	NOW
Unimportant	When Convenient	ASAP

The Eisenhower Matrix.

The Eisenhower Matrix relies on two independent dimensions: urgency and importance. *Urgency* is the sense of pressure that time, or lack thereof, creates. *Importance* has to do with the perceived value of something, monetary or otherwise. Consider each axis independently.

Whether something is more or less important is highly dependent on the situation or context, as well as the perspective of the people involved with it. Typically, the level of importance revolves around how much value is being created, delivered, preserved (saved), captured (collected), or destroyed. But you can just as easily consider it to be the alignment with principles, overarching goals, or ability to advance strategic objectives.

Assuming that *value* is easily measurable, the level of importance will be less subjective than the degree of urgency. To that end, the guidelines that follow offer a useful way to help you quantify the urgency of an item as a potential priority. You can use the Eisenhower Matrix to put items into four buckets: urgent and important; important but not urgent; urgent but not important; and not urgent or important.

Urgent and Important

Some situations are screaming for your attention *right now*—an alarming crisis, a time-sensitive opportunity, or a problem with complex, cascading ramifications downstream. If this is the situation you find yourself in, do what you need to do: react fast and deal with the results afterward.

If it looks like there's not enough time to prioritize explicitly (that is, apply all five phases of DEGAP), one useful option is to turn to a confidante, trusted advisor, or informed leader for additional perspective. Ideally, find someone who knows enough about the situation to give you useful and actionable insights or other relevant advice.

This is key. As discussed at the beginning of this chapter, everybody has priorities whether they're conscious of them or not. Each person's priorities focus their attention on what matters most *to them*, given the information they have at the time. That, in turn, influences what *they* would do. But what's important to you may not line up perfectly with what your supervisor or team members believe is most important to them—or you. For example, a customer service representative (CSR) might feel pressured to remediate a customer complaint immediately. However, the supervisor might be aware that the customer in question has a history of abusing returns and refunds.

Even in truly urgent situations (perhaps especially so), keeping an eye on the bigger picture can have a dramatic effect on how well things turn out. Bob Isaacs, former Sunnyvale Public Safety Officer and Hazardous Materials Specialist, suggests using a "spotter," someone whose job it is to stay back from the front lines and keep an eye on overall priorities, so you don't fixate on a localized set of issues and miss what's actually most important.

Important but Not Urgent

"What is important is seldom urgent, and what is urgent is seldom important," said Eisenhower. Pay particular attention to critical needs, symptoms, or leading indicators. Waiting to take the time to prioritize them can cause you to miss valuable opportunities or allow a once-small issue to grow like a kudzu vine, transforming into a larger problem that might have been preventable.

Problems, opportunities, and needs that are high value almost always merit prioritization. When you know something is important, it's essential to figure out how to focus on it instead of everything else that's competing for your time, attention, and resources.

The upside of acting sooner (but without a false sense of urgency) rather than later is that you'll avoid paying opportunity costs and missing out on what could have been. However, there are always trade-offs. Investing time and energy in a prioritization effort, obviously, will take your attention away from other items that might matter a lot, possibly even more. In situations such as these, it's wise to consider the cost of delaying a competing priority. See the Appendix, "Prioritization Methods," for more information on Cost of Delay.

Urgent but Not Important

The most common situations poke at you, demanding your attention but not for very good reasons. And there are times when waiting is the right thing to do. In situations and contexts where it appears that action is required immediately but the importance is hazy, it's worthwhile to determine just how "urgent" the need really is.

Urgent but not important items tend to consume way too much time, attention, and energy in most workplaces. A good example is the onslaught of email, Slack, or other messages that you wake up to every morning. Is it truly important to respond immediately to each minor request you get, no matter how dramatic the sender's tone is? In my experience, the answer is usually no.

Items in this bucket deplete precious resources and eat up the headroom essential to respond to far more important and sometimes unexpected priorities. When you attend to urgent but not important items, you lose out. They suck the oxygen out of the space needed to think creatively and take effective action.

Not Urgent or Important

If a situation is neither urgent nor important, you can probably defer it. But even when things appear that way, it's a good idea to figure out how to keep tabs on them. You don't want them to take you by surprise later. Sometimes, items that fall into this quadrant have the annoying habit of jumping into a different quadrant, becoming urgent at the most inconvenient times.

It's a truism, but all situations change over time. Some change quickly. Others, not so much. So, if you're using the Eisenhower Matrix, remember that the matrix isn't static: priorities shift and change. The contents of the buckets you fill up aren't frozen in time. Mild symptoms left to fester, for instance, may bloom into full-fledged problems you'll be forced to deal with later. So, don't ignore these items. Monitor them. Because, just like banks never make a mistake in your favor, big problems never crop up when they're convenient.

If you are ready to punt the decision to take time to prioritize, ask yourself, "What assumptions am I making about the rate of change over time?" quickly followed by "What could possibly go wrong if things are left to chance?" Give some serious thought to what's truly most important to you, your team, and your organization.

The Situation Checklist

The other way to determine whether a set of circumstances requires active prioritization is the Situation Checklist. It outlines five common high-level scenarios[2] in which it's usually worth going out of your way to get clear about your priorities up front because priorities are inputs to plans and decisions.

Weirdly, the vast majority of people undervalue the power of a simple checklist for avoiding unintended negative consequences.[3] So, if the Eisenhower Matrix doesn't make it obvious whether you need to embrace all five phases of the DEGAP process model, then use the Situation Checklist when you need a quick way to decide if you need to tap the brakes and slow down to be intentional about figuring out what matters most. Ask yourself if your situation fits into any one of the following five circumstances:

- Starting something new of significance
- Making a difficult decision or approaching a necessary ending[4]

---

2. Michael D. Watkins, *The First 90 Days: Proven Strategies for Getting Up to Speed Faster and Smarter*, Updated, Expanded ed. (Boston, MA: Harvard Business Review Press, 2013).
3. Atul Gawande, *The Checklist Manifesto: How to Get Things Right*, read by John Bedford Lloyd (Macmillan Audio, 2009), Audible audiobook, unabr., 6 hrs., 9 min.
4. This term, coined by psychologist and leadership expert Dr. Henry Cloud in his bestseller book *Necessary Endings*, refers to the idea that things you are currently doing may have outlived their usefulness by preventing growth in other areas.

- Launching a turnaround or fixing something essential
- Scaling up or down, preparing for rapid growth or contraction
- Planning related to making crucial progress or sustaining performance levels

If you put a checkmark next to one of the bullets above, chances are that it's time to decide to follow through with the rest of DEGAP. You would probably come to realize this eventually, but by then you might be completely underwater.

How Long Does Prioritizing Take?

Let's assume that you've concluded that following through with DEGAP is appropriate and valuable. The next thing you'll want to consider is how much time and energy it will take to get through the remaining four phases: Engage, Gather, Arrange, and Prioritize. It should probably go without saying, before you commit to *anything*, it's incumbent upon you to know what you're committing to. Here's what you'll want to consider.

What's the level of urgency and complexity? The higher the level of urgency, the greater the need for a tighter timebox. And greater complexity tends to drive the need for a more methodical (longer) approach. Is your situation a one-off or part of an ongoing effort? You'll want to budget a bit more time for one-off efforts. There might not be an opportunity to "fix it in the mix," as recording engineers like to say, or to adjust priorities later. How many stakeholders are involved: just you, a team, or a larger organization? What kinds of stakeholders are involved? More stakeholders and a greater diversity of people demand a more careful, thoughtful approach. Rushing through things with a false sense of urgency leads to poor outcomes. And finally, what's the overall scope of the effort? As the number of people, places, activities, processes, and information sources rise, so does the need to go slowly at first. Steering clear of avoidable pitfalls helps speed things up as momentum grows.

So, when you decide to embark on a prioritization voyage, what are you getting into? Obviously, this depends on whether you're working solo, as part of a team, or in a larger organization. It also depends on whether you're multitasking. In other words, is it possible to prioritize over time, in between other tasks? Or will it be full brakes on everything else while you focus solely on the prioritization process? The most time-intensive aspect of DEGAP is the Gather phase. This means if high-value information is likely to be hard to come by or inaccessible, plan to spend a bit longer.

The shortest application of the remaining four steps—Engage, Gather, Arrange, and Prioritize—typically consists of a single person working on an episodic prioritization effort. In my experience, this can be expected to require about an hour. A single team, depending on its size and composition, typically needs at least a couple of hours, up to a full day. At the extreme end, an international, multiteam effort, assessing a complex project, can require a few weeks to a couple of months.

To be sure, timing and duration vary greatly, depending on the size and complexity of your organization. The main variable is the amount of time it takes to accurately determine your as-is state and desired future state.

Making the Go/No-Go Decision

Once you've considered the context, urgency, and importance of your situation, and determined how much time you have, making the go/no go decision is relatively straightforward.

Ultimately, people decide to prioritize the process of prioritization when the gap between a given circumstance and the possibility of a better future outcome outweigh the pain they imagine that prioritizing will cause. The "pain" might be having to backburner other things, or the "pain" of the process itself—communicating with stakeholders, making potentially unpopular decisions, or having to give up a pet project.

If it's just you who needs to decide, then be terribly honest with yourself. If you're part of a team that's considering what to do, know this: there's a chance some team member will be adamant there isn't enough time to reflect on priorities or that it's a waste of time. Sometimes, this may be true. But most of the time, such an argument simply reveals an overdeveloped bias toward action or, in some cases, exposes a limiting belief that doing something—*anything*—is more valuable than stepping back and deliberating. This kind of resistance usually highlights the person's lack of understanding about how valuable prioritization is, what's required to do it properly, or both.

Sure, spend too much time prioritizing, and there's a real chance you'll lose control of the timeline. However, not focusing enough on the early phase increases the odds that you'll get trapped in an undesirable timeline—one that you could have avoided by making earlier intentional choices. Your team might deliver something but miss the mark. The question is, by how much? If the answer is, "a lot, potentially," that should be a sufficient sign that it's worth prioritizing prioritization.

In matrixed teams or larger organizations, prioritization is usually initiated by someone in an authority role (a CEO, founder, administrator, VP, or operational leader) who recognizes the need to create a bridge to a more desirable set of outcomes. In these types of situations, whoever accepts responsibility for completing the remainder of the process D(EGAP) is accountable for making sure that there's enough time to do it.

Sometimes making the decision to prioritize explicitly makes it clear that only a one-off effort is necessary. Other times, it points to the need for periodic practice. This involves revisiting your process and continually reprioritizing, depending on the rate of change in each environment. It also means refreshing priorities with new items and information as it becomes available, all the while adjusting existing current priorities to make room for new ones.

With the go/no-go decision behind you, in theory it's time to move on to the next step in the DEGAP process, the Engage phase. However, if you're not in position to do this, then the first step is to figure out how to create the extra space required to be more planful. You'll first want to ease the pressure or constraints of the current situation so that you, your team, or organization can fit prioritization into the mix. Figuring out how to buy yourself breathing room will result in the thing that prevents you from being boxed in such a stressful situation to begin with.

4

Engage in
the Process

With the go/no-go decision behind you, you've progressed to the next step in the DEGAP process, which means that you've determined that being intentional about prioritization is viable and feasible, given time and resource restraints.

The "E" in DEGAP means to engage in the prioritization process in a purposeful way. The function of this step is to connect your decision to action. It asks you to carve out the time and space to follow the remainder of the process workflow, identify the people who could potentially influence (or be influenced by) the prioritization process (aka stakeholders), and identify essential sources of information.

DEGAP: Engage phase.

As you move into this phase, try your best to cultivate an open mind. A sense of curiosity and a willingness to face the reality of your current circumstances as they actually are, rather than what you think they "should" be, will serve you well. This approach takes perseverance and courage: the emotional courage to face hard truths, the intellectual courage to cope with complexity and ambiguity, the social courage to handle difficult conversations, the ethical courage to do the right thing, and just plain physical courage to keep pushing when you're out of steam.

Create Time and Space

As touched on in the previous chapter, the total amount of time you'll end up needing depends on a lot of different variables. Regardless, you'll want to start every effort off on the right foot.

Shove away interruptions and distractions so that you can focus. For one-off prioritization efforts, see if you can find a place to work until you've completed all the tasks that are part of the DEGAP process—a place where you can spread out without being disrupted, annoyed, or harassed. If you're working from home, avoid working where a cat can (and will) sit on your papers or laptop. Cats have evolved to be *the* priority.

For periodic (habitual) prioritization, the most basic way to do this is to schedule short blocks of time in your calendar, say 30 minutes a few times a week at first. Scheduling time with yourself to stare off into space may seem silly. But it's a proven hack for creating time to be proactive, rather than pushing forward blindly, relying on the (likely false) hope that you'll magically find some unclaimed time in the future.

If you work in an office, look for a dedicated space that you can reserve and where you will not be disturbed until you're done. A conference table is great so long as you won't be forced to pick up and move while everything is all spread out. Large whiteboards and glass windows are also nice as long as they won't be erased or stripped of Post-it notes. For ongoing prioritization efforts, it's less about the physical space itself and more about protecting your time to think.

For individuals, I recommend picking a time first thing in the morning or, alternatively, later in the evening when interruptions will be at a minimum. See Chapter 9 for more information. If you're part of a team or need input from different parts of your organization, though, finding time is obviously going to be more difficult. Planning responsibility naturally falls to senior leaders, who must establish a cadence where business units, divisions, departments, and teams can synchronize their efforts across the organizational hierarchy. Not surprisingly, if engaging involves lots of people, it will take longer and must be managed more methodically than an effort requiring just a few folks or an intact team. This is okay.

My advice is to roll with the punches, saving your concerns and brainpower for the final step in the DEGAP process, Prioritize. Now, let's meet your stakeholders.

Meet Your Stakeholders

Next, it's time to engage your stakeholders. Stakeholders are the people who have an interest (a *stake*) in what priorities you choose and the results you get, as well as any unintended consequences that spring from your decision(s). This cohort may include work colleagues, bosses, customers, suppliers, and community members. Or, if your decision is more personal in nature, it could include family members and friends as well.

Stakeholders have a lot to offer. They can help you anticipate potential problems or solutions that you haven't already considered. They can also shed light on the impact of your prioritization choices: consequences, constraints, and other factors that will inform the priorities you, your team, or your organization ultimately settle on. Not to mention, when stakeholders feel like they're heard, they'll generally be more supportive of an outcome borne from a prioritization process, even if it turns out to be a negative one.

The best practice is to communicate with stakeholders as early as possible in your planning process. The later you learn something, the less of an opportunity you'll have to respond to what you've learned. So, seriously, don't wait: early insights and information have a compounding effect. They grow potentially more valuable over time.[1]

The last thing you want is to end up debating the finalized priorities after you've already completed all five steps in the DEGAP process. Once you've invested a lot of time and energy into figuring things out, you definitely don't want to discover that you missed talking to key people or overlooked other important sources of information.

1. Darren Hardy, *The Compound Effect: Multiply Your Success One Simple Step at a Time* (Folio Literary Management, 2019), Audible audiobook, unabr., 4 hrs., 44 min.

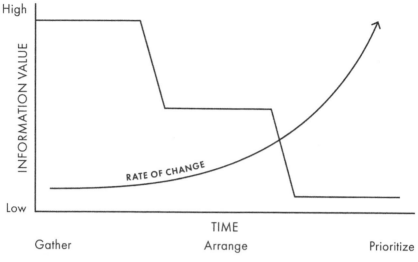

Value of information over time.

The longer you wait to get stakeholders involved, the more momentum you'll have to overcome, which can create a hazard. It becomes increasingly difficult to slow down and back up if necessary.

The activity of collecting perspectives, comments, shared experiences, diverse points of view, and other reference points will form the foundation of the third phase: Gather. Plus, the more involved your stakeholders are from the beginning to the end of the DEGAP process, the more committed they'll be when it comes to executing the ultimate priorities.

Make Peace with Your Internal Stakeholders

Here's a curveball: the term *stakeholder* typically refers to other human beings, both outside and inside an organization. But it's also useful to imagine that you have personal internal stakeholders as well. These are distinctive and inseparable parts of yourself: voices in your head (but in a healthy way) that represent your needs, wants, interests, goals, and worries, or major roles that you play in other people's lives.

Identifying internal mental stakeholders, labeling them (e.g., my inner CFO, as a husband or wife, or the rebel in me), and then gathering information from them by listening to what they have to say is a profoundly useful way to stay aware of "who" needs to be involved in terms of driving the process forward. Ultimately, making these stakeholders an explicit part of your process can help you navigate through DEGAP that much more smoothly.

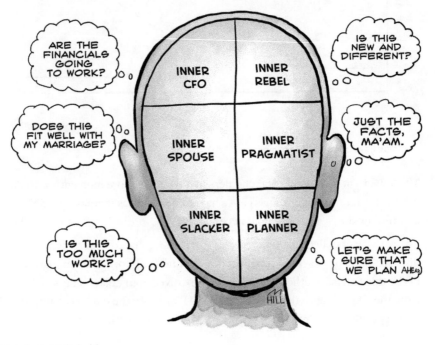

Inner stakeholders.

Once you have time allotted and your stakeholders on board, you can move forward to the next step: Gather. This is the part of DEGAP where you pinpoint items and relevant information about them.

5

Gather Items
to Prioritize

There's a nearly seamless transition from the previous task of engaging in the process to actively gathering information about your current circumstances and desired outcomes.

Gathering is detective work. It's the task of investigating what matters and why. It's soliciting input from the stakeholders you just identified. It involves digging up items to consider prioritizing, uncovering important information about those items, and discovering insights that could turn out to be pivotal when it comes time to winnow them down and arrange them in order of importance (i.e., prioritize).

DEGAP: Gather phase.

Characterize Challenges and Opportunities

The activity of gathering items is informed by the circumstances that surround the gap between a current and desired state. The assumption behind the Gather phase is that stakeholders have a common understanding that there is, in fact, a challenge or opportunity worth pursuing.

This can take many forms—an inspiring mission, a North Star goal, a compelling objective, a well-designed strategy, or a highly desirable outcome. So, before you begin talking to stakeholders in earnest, you'll want to give some thought to what you believe the main problem (or opportunity) is. And you'll want to reflect on the desired outcome. Doing so will help frame the situation and establish the reason behind and the need to gather, arrange, and eventually prioritize items.

Seems easy, right? However, "problem" is an overloaded term. It means different things to different people, depending on their circumstances. Here, a *problem* represents a situation that people want to *get away from*. While an *opportunity* is a circumstance that people want *to move toward*.

So, for our purposes, consider problem, opportunity, and challenge to mean roughly the same thing, in other words, a gap between a condition or current state and an expected, desired, or required state. To simplify matters and inspired by Richard Rumelt who wrote the book, *The Crux*, going forward, I will use the word *challenge*[1] instead of problem or opportunity.

Understand the Current State

Understanding the current state requires you to gather information about the context of the problem, the people who are involved with or touched by the problem, and any issues around timing:

- **Context:** This is the venue, the problem space, or the circumstance responsible for the gap. The context establishes a kind of boundary condition or imaginary bubble that surrounds a given problem or opportunity. Every situation and context suggest a set of needs and wants. In other words, the situation and context inform what's likely to be most and least important. For example, the challenges associated with a family reunion are wildly different from those related to a business offsite. And the kinds of challenges related to a business offsite are quite distinct from a research symposium.

- **People:** This represents the number and locations of people who are (or might be) affected by the problem and their ability to communicate to resolve it. This element can encompass the locales, languages, cultures, and any other essential differences that you need to consider, including access to the internet and other technologies.

- **Timing:** This involves the temporal constraints determining the speed, sequencing, and how formal/methodical (or quick-and-dirty) the process is. Timing also influences who needs to be involved and when (will people work asynchronously, in parallel, or serially?), as well as the speed

---

1. Richard P. Rumelt, *The Crux: How Leaders Become Strategists*, read by Richard P. Rumelt (PublicAffairs, 2022), Audible audiobook, unabr., 10 hrs., 53 min.

with which people need to be engaged in the problem-solving process, communications, and acceptable response times.

Gathering information about the current state provides orientation. It answers the questions "Where are we?" and "How did we get here?"

Gathering is detective work.

When you are ready to talk to stakeholders, sometimes it's helpful to ground the conversation with facts as you see them. So, first start with yourself and then shift to others. Ask yourself things like, "What's the situation from my vantage point?"; "How much time do we have?"; "How did we get here?"; or "Where are we now?" Knowing where you stand provides a stronger foundation for asking others what they think.

Clarify the Preferred State or Desired Outcome

As explained, the gap between the current "as-is" state and a desired future state depends on what's needed, wanted, expected, or required. This means that it's essential to have a crystal-clear understanding of what it is you're working toward (i.e., your desired outcome). If you're not completely sure of this—and many definitely aren't—one helpful way to figure it out is to work through the Desired Outcome model that follows, which John Grinder and

Richard Bandler developed.[2] The model consists of six pointed questions engineered to elicit clarifying responses.

If you want to increase the likelihood that your efforts will yield more of what you want (and less of what you don't), answer these questions candidly. Because "It's only when you know what you're doing that you can really do what you want."[3]

Desired Outcome Model Questions

1. **What do you want?** Silicon Valley consultant types call this the *presenting request*. The healthcare industry refers to it as the *chief complaint*. And academics use the term *objective*. This question represents an explicit want or need.

2. **What's even more important (the meta outcome)?** Rarely does the initial request get to the heart of what's truly needed. Instead, this is generally hidden under the surface. This question highlights the value that's deeper than the presenting request. It helps bring to the surface the answer to the deeper question of why the presenting request is wanted or needed. It aims to get to the underlying reasons, deeper benefits, or higher-level intent. It's the real goal.

3. **What is the evidence for success?** The evidence is the yardstick that measures whether "the want" and the "meta outcome" get satisfied. The evidence is the rubric for measuring success—specifically, how you will know when *what's wanted* has been achieved. The evidence is real and objective, not imaginary—it must be measurable and tangible: things you see, hear, or touch. Your proposed evidence may be barely sufficient or hopelessly idealistic. It's on you to find out which.

4. **What are the obstacles to success?** Obstacles are constraints or conditions that stand in the way of success. Defining them helps shape the approach to delivering a desired outcome. To knock them down, work around, or deal with them effectively, obstacles need to be surfaced, properly framed, and appropriately mitigated or solved. In effect, obstacles are the real or perceived reasons that you don't already have

2. Richard Bandler and John Grinder, *Frogs into Princes: Neuro Linguistic Programming* (Moab, UT: Real People Press, 1979).
3. Moshe Feldenkrais, *The Master Moves* (Capitola, CA: Meta Publications, 1984).

or might be thwarted from getting what you want. Sometimes the only sensible answer to this question is simply acknowledging that a solution simply does not exist (yet!). Alternatively, a correct answer may be that it does exist, but isn't accessible.

5. **What are the potential negative unintended consequences?** When you solve one problem, you often create new ones. Sometimes these new problems are insignificant or take time to manifest. Other times they are massive and immediate. Asking questions about potential unintended negative consequences helps you see reality for what *it is*, not what it *should* be. Go out of your way to get different perspectives, especially those from people of different backgrounds. Investing the time and energy to surface potential problems before they manifest allows you to plan for ways to mitigate them before you lose control of the timeline.

6. **What are the steps to success?** No doubt you've heard the famous Chinese proverb that says a journey of a thousand miles begins with a single step. True that. But there's a critical question that precedes that first step: "Is there a step before the first step?" There often is. The answers are often surprising and revealing. Don't skip this step.

Remember, again, that every gap equals the distance between the current state and a future state. So, the more successful you are at gathering facts and opinions about your as-is situation and your desired outcome, the better equipped you'll be to construct a solid bridge of well-informed items . . . aka potential priorities.

Use a Gathering System

Talking to stakeholders and investigating sources of truth generate both qualitative and quantitative data. It's the most effective way to amass the information you need to close a gap and to better understand what the criteria are for future success.

The principal tools for gathering information are listening effectively and notetaking. Both are essential because very often information gets distorted, deleted, or generalized[4] as it moves from the source, through your ears to your brain, and into your conscious awareness. "Your brain is not a tape

---

4. Bandler and Grinder, *Frogs into Princes*.

recorder, and your ear is not a microphone," says Nelson Pass, the "spiritual leader" of the DIY audiophile community and president of Pass Labs.[5] That's why you need to be deliberate when you listen and take notes.

So, as you gather information, listen carefully. Listening is simultaneously one of the easiest and the most vexing things to do well. In my experience, it's the single most important general-purpose skill in your toolbox. It's one thing to "hear" what people are telling you. It's another thing altogether to really internalize important points and even specific words.

One effective way to ensure that you understand what your stakeholders are saying and integrate their concerns into the process is to paraphrase or even repeat what you heard. The ability to play back verbatim what somebody said to you is a powerful technique with multiple benefits: Not only does it force you to pay acute attention in the moment, preventing you from worrying about what you are going to say next, but it also increases your precision by allowing you to confirm your understanding. Plus, it signals that you are paying attention, which helps ensure that people feel heard and, as a result, respected.

Take Good Notes

The task of gathering is not only to come up eventually with a set of items (potential priorities) to be evaluated. Rather, the goal here is to build a pile of illuminating information, both qualitative and quantitative: notes, quotes, audio/video recordings, drawings, interview transcripts, etc. What you do with that information will help you determine the priorities and the quality of them. This is where interviews and good notetaking come in.

As you talk to stakeholders and capture potential priorities, make sure that you also jot down relevant metadata. Metadata are tidbits of information about each item that might turn out to be useful later. A straightforward example of metadata relates to a document like this book.

A reader is far more likely to be interested in the contents of the book than the metadata about the book, which includes the genre, author, imprint (publisher), ISBN, publication date, page count, and title. For potential priorities,

---

5. Used with permission by Nelson Pass.

you'll want to capture any data about the item that is likely to help you distinguish items and evaluate them against one another.

Metadata for items might include the source or originator, logical owner, stakeholders, approximate scope (size), date/time it was collected, the context(s) in which it applies, and other pertinent categories. For instance, is it a bug or a feature (of a product)? Capturing metadata along with potential priorities helps ensure that the information you gather remains distinguishable and easily understandable after multiple conversations, which might otherwise blur together in your mind.

For teams and groups, there are different ways to coordinate the gathering process. Some people are more comfortable using virtual documents, spreadsheets, or whiteboards. Others would rather use digital card-based applications. The most demanding environments, particularly those within larger organizations, will benefit from the use of a collaboration platform such as one that is purpose-built for prioritization.

Regardless of whether you're working by yourself, on a team, or as part of a larger organization, the simple act of capturing items and other essential information, distilling it down, and seeing it all in one place begins to reveal what's more—rather than less—important. Once you have your notecards (or digital equivalent), congrats: you have your first items.

Select Different Kinds of Items

As you go about gathering information, scan for all kinds of items, not just the obvious types such as projects, tasks, or action items. People, places, things, activities, information, and time are the top-level categories. They comprise:

- **People:** Categories of people, groups, or constituencies
- **Places:** Locations, both real and virtual: sites, queues, etc.
- **Things:** Material things, virtual, or imaginary objects: products, services, tools, etc.
- **Activities:** Projects, initiatives, actions, and tasks
- **Information:** Any type of data at any level of abstraction, quantifiable or subjective: goals, objectives, ideas, values, complaints, symptoms, needs, questions, risk factors, etc.
- **Time:** Processes: phases, workflows, sequencing, system effects, and transitions

Maintaining an awareness of the diverse range of potential priorities will help ensure that you don't miss important buckets of items.

Here's where all that metadata you recorded can help you. Being able to clearly view an item's attributes, properties, commonalities, categories, and other metadata will make it that much easier to put them in appropriate buckets and evaluate them against one another. Better information will lead to a stronger analysis.

Comprehensive metadata will also allow you to filter, sort, or view items in flexible ways. With a bit of scrutiny, you'll be able to see how some items might be more important than others.

As you gather items, note any unifying criteria, conceptual themes, or dimensions that are relevant to the item. Common examples include the amount of *effort* an item might require, the *impact* (positive or negative value) an item might have, the *size* or *scope* of an item, or the relevant *time horizon* (e.g., now, later, or future).

If possible, also take stock of more advanced attributes, such as static versus dynamic complexity, cognitive complexity, or time-constancy assumptions. And pay particular attention to direct dependencies among items, as well as items that represent leverage points—items that if tackled upstream could have a disproportionate effect on others downstream.

Distinguish Good Items vs. Bad Items

Every item has the potential to become a priority. But the quality of a given item depends on how carefully crafted it happens to be. And it isn't too hard to tell a good and useful item from a bad or less useful one. In this context *good* and *bad* connote the quality of the description of the item, not whether the item itself is good or bad.

Good items are self-evident, mutually exclusive, and easy to compare against one another. It should be obvious what they are. Their labels or descriptions are specific and concrete. Bad items are vague, abstract, and imprecise. You may not be quite sure what you're dealing with—or into what buckets an item should fall.

Good items also need to include at least one, but preferably two or more attributes, like "cost," and values like "high, medium, low" associated with those attributes. Together, these properties allow items to be judged more or less importantly relative to one another. Although it's possible to use brute force to (attempt to) prioritize items with poor or minimal information about those items, the more (and better) information you have about each item, the easier it will be to arrange them in order of importance when the time comes.

6

Arrange Items and Related Information

At some point, you'll notice that you're running out of stakeholders to talk to and sources of truth to investigate. You'll also realize that you've gathered a lot of helpful raw data about challenges and opportunities, as well as stakeholder needs and wants. Perhaps your list of potential priorities is growing sizably.

If this is where you find yourself, it probably means it's time to move on to the "A" in DEGAP: Arrange. This is the time to review and clean up your potential priorities and the information about those items you've collected in preparation for the last task of the process, prioritizing. You'll do that (prioritize) using frameworks, sorting techniques, simulations, or hybrid techniques, all of which are specially equipped to compare items against one another. But I digress.

Arranging what you've gathered thus far involves clarifying even further what each item is and, as much as possible, quantifying its relative value. The goal is to make each item even more obvious and understandable, to normalize and demystify it, to remove remaining vagueness or ambiguity. Ultimately, the value of each item (or lack thereof) starts to become obvious at this point.

DEGAP: Arrange phase.

This process is analogous to mining for diamonds. Finding diamonds in the wild presents one challenge; preparing them for market is another one altogether. After you find a raw diamond, you still have a lot of work to do to create the polished facets that will make each diamond beautiful, special, and valuable.

So how do you get from a big pile of information rocks to a sifted list of prioritizable items? You start by giving yourself time to reflect on what, thus far, has been collected. You not only scrutinize potential items, but also criteria, constraints, and other important considerations (dependencies, critical open questions, or previously hidden assumptions that may have surfaced). Spread them out in front of you. You might want to use an online visual collaboration platform. Alternatively, 3x5 Post-it notes on a whiteboard or index cards on a large conference table also work.

Next, massage the information you've gathered. Delete items that are obviously repetitive and clear up potential confusion by further refining vague language or ambiguities. "Most people aren't suspicious of language, but it directs everything,"[1] according to Dan French, Master Rhetorician and Emmy-nominated Hollywood comedy writer.

You don't want items that might be related but in some difficult-to-discern and undefined way; they're either related or they're not. If they are related, figure out how to tie them together, possibly by merging them. If they aren't, then make sure they are different, distinct, and separate. Fuzzy or poorly defined items will end up making the prioritization process less fun for sure, and they will make the DEGAP process that much more difficult in the long run.

Before you begin sorting individual items, you'll also want to identify dependencies and commitments. Look for items that are tightly coupled to existing commitments or ones that are causally linked to other items.

A more advanced subtask is to hunt for leverage points. Do any of the items function as keystones or logical parents in a hierarchy of other items? I'm talking about the kinds of items that, if they were addressed, would naturally resolve a cascade of others. Try to keep track of how items are logically related to one another, especially at higher or lower levels of abstraction, such as parent/child relationships.

Finally, if you're working with others, this is also the time to discuss and debate your findings. Is everyone on board with how the items are organized? Is there a way to refine them even further? Would you be better off with more, or maybe fewer, categories or buckets? Work through any differences of opinion as best you can. Everything doesn't have to be perfect before you move on, but people should be in general agreement.

Criteria, Constraints, and Dimensions

When there are more than three criteria by which to evaluate an item, and the number of potential priorities is large—say, greater than 25—the challenge quickly becomes how to choose efficiently and select wisely. Fredkin's

---

1. Used with permission by Dan French.

Paradox states that the more similar options are, the more difficult it will be and the longer it will take to choose among them. So, dealing with this is important.

For an item to be compared and contrasted to other items in a meaningful way, each one must be unique and distinguishable. Each should have characteristics, attributes, and other properties that will make it more or less important relative to other items. These properties include criteria, constraints, or dimensions that permit you to assign values to them.

For instance, imagine that one of your stakeholders proposes developing a major new feature for a flagship product. As a result, when you've gathered items related to that feature, you'll also want to have captured ancillary information and metadata about each item. This could include the source of the item, the amount of value it provides, the level of effort and cost it would take to develop it, any dependencies it might have, and, of course, how essential or useful it would be to customers.

In product development, *impact* and *effort* are two standard dimensions that reflect the value of developing a new feature or capability. *Impact* is the amount of benefit to be gained; *effort* is the amount of work required. On their own, impact and effort are just raw attributes of a given feature or capability. Both are terrifically useful once values are linked to them. It can be an ordinal value such as high, medium, or low impact or effort, or you can use something more exacting.

Use a Scale to Differentiate Items

One thing to be aware of, although it's not a rigid rule, is that when you eventually rank or sort (arrange) items in order of importance, you usually need to consider two or more criteria or dimensions to compare them meaningfully. So, how do you do this? You use a meaningful scale.

To compare items to one another, you will need to use some sort of scale to differentiate their criteria or dimensions. There are three classes of scales that you can use. Ranging from easy to difficult, and qualitatively fuzzy to quantitatively precise, they are as follows: ordinal scales, ratio scales, and absolute scales.

The simplest and easiest way to compare items against each other is to use is an ordinal scale (high, medium, low; 1, 2, 3; etc.). The downside is that these scales don't let you see how much more important one item is over another. Given any three items, for example, the value of the first item might be 10 times more important than the middle item, and 1,000 times more than the third one. Picture a mosquito, T-Rex, and a Boeing 737.

A.) MOSQUITO→ ·

B.) T-REX

C.) BOEING 737

Ordinal vs. ratio scales.

Moreover, if you choose to rate things only in terms of relative importance—A, B, C, D, E, F—you will not be in a strong position to defend the arrangement with math to your stakeholders or boss.

Ordinal scales are popular (and tend to be overused) because of how simple they are. However, ordinal scales pose certain challenges that aren't easy to overcome in any sufficiently complex environment (say, a fully engaged prioritization effort). They are highly subjective, idiosyncratic, and rarely evidence based.

If you seek greater clarity, you will be better off exploiting a ratio scale such as the Fibonacci sequence, where numbers increase at larger intervals. The Fibonacci sequence helps people see meaningful differences of values among items. Put simply, without the Fibonacci sequence, two items that are close in value, can essentially end up appearing to be the same value. So the Fibonacci sequence helps you avoid the all-too-human tendency to pretend that you can accurately differentiate between minor but potentially critical differences in value.

Ratio scales like the Fibonacci sequence utilize a spectrum of value (e.g., 1–144). Ratio scales help address the core limitations of ordinal-scale approaches because they let you see how much more important, valuable, etc., one item is than another.

Interestingly, you can also use the Fibonacci sequence to help with relative estimation and thus avoid the planning fallacy.[2] This is the phenomena where humans tend to underestimate what it will take to accomplish something over time. Humans are biased to be overly optimistic about what it will actually take to get a job done.

Under other circumstances you may want to employ an absolute scale, which requires calculating or assigning a definitive number to items—for example, monetary value. Using an absolute scale is often appropriate in prioritization efforts where stakeholders are seeking more quantifiable answers, calculations are defensible, and understanding the decision logic might be helpful after the fact. For more information on probability fields and estimates of value, check out *How to Measure Anything: Finding the Value of Intangibles in Business*[3] by Douglas W. Hubbard. Half-jokingly, Doug once said to me, "I didn't write a book on how to measure most things. I wrote a book on how to measure anything." The chapter on calibrated estimation is worth the price of the book alone.

Once you have decided which scale(s) to use to weigh the value of your priorities; considered the criteria, constraints, and dimensions of the items you've gathered; and otherwise arranged your items in a way that's logical and makes comparing like to like easy, you are ready for the next step.

It's time to prioritize.

2. Daniel Kahneman and Amos Tversky, *Intuitive Prediction: Biases and Corrective Procedures,* archived PDF from the original on September 8, 2013. (Decision Research Technical Report PTR-1042-77-6, 1977).
3. Douglas W. Hubbard, *How to Measure Anything: Finding the Value of Intangibles in Business* (Hoboken, NJ: John Wiley & Sons, 2007).

CHAPTER

7

Prioritize Items

I f you've made it to this point, you've decided that the benefits of being intentional about prioritizing outweigh the opportunity costs of not focusing or working on something else.

You've engaged in the process in a conscious way, identifying essential sources of information and communicating with stakeholders. And you've gathered and arranged the information and items that need to be prioritized. Now it's time to begin prioritizing the items.

If you're working solo, you'll be able to approach prioritizing in the most straightforward way possible. If you're part of a team, however, you'll need to take a wider perspective. This means opening the door as wide as possible to include additional stakeholders and gather more items as needed. You will also need to take a deeper look at your current circumstances. And if more than one team is involved in the prioritization process, your approach will need to be even more refined.

Fear not, though, you can do this. I've helped a plethora of leaders and employees through this process. Because that's what it ultimately is—a process.

DEGAP: Prioritize phase.

The most successful organizations expect their teams to be able to translate higher-level strategies or key priorities into practical priorities for themselves. And those teams, in turn, rely on their individual members to keep their priorities straight.

That means it's 100 percent on you to figure out what your role in the process is. Is it your job alone? Or do you need to be an active participant on a team? If you're a participant, then what aspects of the process are you responsible for? Are you taking an active role in running the process or are you simply a stakeholder in the process and eventual outcome? These are all important questions to consider before you dive in and begin prioritizing.

Choose an Approach to Prioritizing

When you prioritize for yourself and by yourself, often the easiest approach is to use a popular framework such as the Eisenhower Matrix introduced in Chapter 3, which pits the dimension of urgency against the opposing dimension of importance. Alternatively, you can use a simple sorting technique such as Stack Ranking covered in Chapter 8 or Pareto Analysis, commonly known as the *80/20 rule*, which is one of the simplest, most universally applicable methods. See the Appendix for more information on these and other common approaches to prioritization.

The two common objectives of a solo prioritization effort are to manage tasks, projects, or to-do lists more effectively; or to plan or make a decision about something that will have long-term ramifications. And these two frameworks provide a good place to start.

However, in situations where you are creating plans or making big decisions, you'll get better results if you define your desired outcome first. Getting clear about how you want things to turn out ultimately gives you a sharp lens through which decisions are based. And this will inform your priorities. See Chapter 8 for detailed instructions on how to spell out a desired outcome.

As discussed, prioritizing becomes more complicated when it involves working with a group of people, whether on a team or within a larger organization. In addition to the prioritization process itself, to facilitate effective collaboration you may need to work through a host of unique considerations: locale, language, time zones, tooling, and techniques. Decision rights may also have to be managed.

But before you decide which approach to use, you need to understand the pros and cons of each. If you're a member of a team, the context and situation will largely determine the required approach. For instance, the needs of a product design group are quite different from the needs of a medical team. The needs of an IT cybersecurity team are quite different from a NASA launch-planning team. For these kinds of teams, frameworks and sorting techniques may not be enough on their own. The situation may call for a simulation or a hybrid approach.

Finally, if you are playing in a larger organization, the size and scope of a prioritization effort will have a big impact on the approach that is best. In these situations, the most common scenario involves a team of teams driving toward decisions, plans, or strategies.

So how do you know whether to use a visual framework, a sorting technique, a simulation, or a hybrid approach? The annoying answer is that *it depends*. The dimensions you choose or criteria you use to assess items under consideration depend fundamentally on the context of the prioritization effort. For instance, in the context of a for-profit business, increasing the business value is typically the overarching need that informs your choices. But "business value" can be expressed in many different ways: in terms of making money, saving money, avoiding unnecessary costs, achieving mission-critical goals, acquiring and retaining talent, increasing market or wallet share, or brand awareness. You get the idea.

Next, I'll provide a brief overview of the various approaches. This includes the kind of frameworks, sorting techniques, simulations, and hybrid methods you'll encounter in the chapters that follow.

Visual Frameworks

Frameworks illustrate concepts that are difficult to envision using words alone. By creating a mental canvas for comparing and contrasting items or other important factors to prioritize against one another, frameworks can be powerful thinking tools. They provide form and structure to what might be an important but otherwise abstract or unwieldy idea. They allow you to see hidden dimensions and offer insightful perspectives.

Different frameworks call out the important dimensions of a concept and help create shared understanding. You should use a framework when seeing a visual relationship among choices in order to put things in perspective.

Frameworks come in different shapes and sizes. Some are simple "Small-F" frameworks. Often deceptively simple, these popular frameworks rely on a two-by-two matrix. Their goal is to distill what's important down to two or three generally applicable dimensions. For example, the ever-popular Eisenhower Matrix introduced in Chapter 3 pits the dimension of urgency against the opposing dimension of importance.

In contrast, "Big-F" frameworks, such as the Max Priorities Pyramid (introduced in Chapter 12), require explanation and instruction to be useful. But there are hundreds of powerful frameworks, and new ones are continuing to be invented as new needs present themselves. See the Appendix for a list of the most commonly used ones, which are described throughout this book.

If it's possible to use a framework, it's a good idea to do so. Frameworks offer an easy way to make sense of the world. They push you to cut out unnecessary detail and cut to the heart of what's at stake. By making it obvious along which dimensions different items stack up relative to one another, frameworks are perfect for clarifying what matters most quickly—and getting people on the same page about it. The visual nature of frameworks simplifies things, making it easier to see the big picture and immediately comprehend important relationships among items. By abstracting away (potentially distracting) details, frameworks present items like points on a map rather than precise GPS coordinates.

Incidentally, you can use more than one framework. You can even feed the output of one into another to filter items through a different set of dimensions for different purposes. This series can produce insights that would probably elude you if you were to use only one framework or another.

If you're working solo, consider starting with the Eisenhower Matrix by default to flush out what's urgent and important. (See Chapter 8.) Or, if you are overwhelmed with the number of items before you, you can "prune" them by trimming less important "branches" or "leaves" using Prune the Product Tree, originally presented in the book *Innovation Games* by Luke Hohmann, coauthor of *Software Profit Streams*™ and Chief Innovation Officer, Applied Frameworks SAFe® Fellow. More recently, it was popularized and renamed (for general use) as Prune the Future in *Gamestorming* by Dave Gray, Sunni Brown, and James Macanufo. Following the metaphor, this can help you redirect your energy toward what you want to grow.

Speedboat is a particularly valuable framework for teams. It employs the metaphor of a motorboat attempting to power through the water with sufficient speed, i.e., if the boat isn't moving fast enough, it won't be able to plane. See Chapter 11 on how to use Speedboat to accelerate team progress.

Similarly, if you're not progressing in your quest to prioritize, you too may find yourself vulnerable to currents and waves that knock you off course. The objectives of this framework are to identify what's impeding progress, anchoring it in place, or lurking dangerously under the surface. Speedboat helps teams see what's slowing things down.

If you work in product design and development, your team may benefit by using two specific frameworks in series, Prune the Product Tree and Impact/Effort Matrix. The former makes clear what is core versus peripheral. Piping the output of Prune the Product Tree into the Impact/Effort Matrix lets a team get a handle on items that will deliver the most bang for their buck.

Larger organizations may struggle more to find an optimal approach. That said, I've found the Max Priorities Pyramid to be a powerful tool for getting multiple teams on the same page about what matters from high-level goals all the way down to more tactical actions. See Chapter 12 for a more detailed explanation of what this framework is, why it's important, and how it works in practice.

Sorting Techniques

In contrast to visual frameworks, which illustrate relationships, sorting techniques give you a more forceful way to surface specific differences among individual items.

Even the simplest sorting techniques require separating this from that based on at least one criterion or judgment. And a decision to value one item over another acknowledges a meaningful difference between two or more items, however small those differences might be. Therefore, in its simplest form, *sorting* is the foundation of *prioritizing*.

If you're prioritizing for yourself by yourself, it's best to start with basic techniques, such as Stack Ranking or Paired Comparison, which are both covered in Chapter 8. Other, more sophisticated approaches are discussed in later chapters of the book and in the Appendix. However, if you're working with a team, you will probably want to use a collaborative technique such as Crawford's Slip Writing method, where members jot down their items on real or virtual paper, or Dot Voting, where people work together to determine relative priority using a nonbinding "vote" represented by a check mark or traffic-light-colored dot in a digital visual collaboration space, whiteboard, or flipchart.[1]

Use a Scorecard (and Maybe a Spreadsheet)

Scorecards let you use numbers to figure out how to rank items you want to prioritize. They're very versatile; they can be simple, qualitative, and manual. Or they can be sophisticated, quantitative, and automated.

It's common to use spreadsheets to create scorecards and calculate priorities. They are particularly useful when you need to evaluate against a set of specific criteria and where values may need to be calculated to explain the relationships among competing items and choices. In addition, spreadsheets let you assign numerical weighting factors to criteria, a crucial step when some criteria are more important than others.

1. Sunni Brown, *The Doodle Revolution*, ill. ed. (New York, NY: Portfolio/Penguin, 2015).

Although scorecards can be useful if you are working on your own, they're really helpful for teams and larger organizations if they're dealing with many items, categories, or other attributes that would otherwise be too unwieldy to manage in a framework or sorting technique. This is key if you want to slice and dice a complex set of items or prioritize them in different ways.

Simulations

A *simulation* is an interactive "game" that gives people a safe place to explore the kinds of conversations, trade-offs, decisions, and actions that would have consequences if they played out in real life, for better or for worse—think Monopoly.

The Buy-a-Feature simulation offers a good example. A team working in a product design and development setting can use Buy a Feature to negotiate how each "player" would "invest" a predetermined amount of fake money to arrive at a list of prioritized features or other requirements. Buy a Feature is another powerful approach from the book *Innovation Games* by Luke Hohmann.

Simulation methods.

Choose a simulation when you find yourself with multiple stakeholders who have a diverse set of needs that need to be negotiated dynamically against one another.

In such a scenario, a simulation can help you produce reliable compromises. As always, active stakeholder participation leads to stronger alignment among all parties.

Hybrid Methods

Some approaches to prioritization do not fit neatly into a single category. I refer to them as *hybrid methods* because they employ various combinations or sequences of different frameworks, sorting techniques, and simulations. Some hybrid methods involve combining or sequencing two or more approaches to yield a better result. For example, Prune the Product Tree and *then* Buy a Feature. Other hybrid approaches are integrated like a hybrid car, where two or more approaches are "chained" together into a single method to accomplish more than the sum of the individual approaches could on their own.

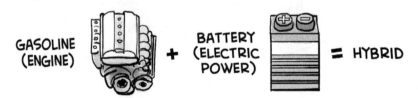

Hybrid methods.

Another example is the Analytic Hierarchy Process (AHP)[2] discussed in Chapter 13. AHP is a robust approach to prioritizing at scale in larger organizations. It is a hybrid method that combines Paired Comparison with a quantitative approach to the Impact/Effort Matrix for adjudicating conflicting criteria. It's typically used to address large-scale, multiparty, multicriteria prioritization challenges, making it especially relevant for strategic or annual planning. But I digress. Let's get back to selecting an approach.

Selecting an Approach

It's important to settle on an approach that best fits your circumstances. In my experience, your choice depends on two key elements:

- **People:** The number and locations of people involved in the decision-making process (including stakeholders who might be affected by the outcomes of focusing on certain priorities over others) is extremely important to consider. Their access (or lack of access) to good communication technology also matters, as do the languages of the people involved and any other essential differences, cultural or otherwise. Put simply, how complicated will it be to communicate quickly and clearly?

- **Time and space:** How quickly do you need to prioritize and how much time do you have to do it? This constrains your choices. The temporal boundaries directly affect the speed, sequencing, and formality of the priority-making process. Time and temporal boundaries also influence who might need to be involved and when (asynchronous or serially), as well as the speed with which people need to be engaged in the process and how quickly action must be taken.

Once you have a sense of the effort's scope, you can determine how rigorous the prioritizing effort needs to be. This is the point at which you can seriously consider whether to use visual frameworks, sorting techniques, a hybrid method, or a combination of approaches.

---

2. Originally developed by Prof. Thomas L. Saaty (July 18, 1926–August 14, 2017) a Distinguished University Professor at the University of Pittsburgh, Graduate School of Business.

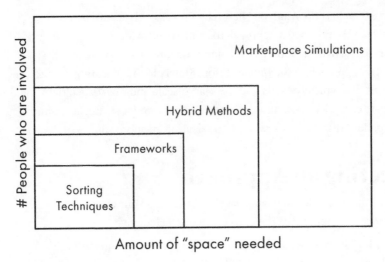

Selecting an approach.

After you have a sense of the effort's scope, you can determine how rigorous the prioritizing effort needs to be. This is the point at which you can seriously consider whether to use visual frameworks, sorting techniques, a hybrid method, or a combination of approaches.

From Theory to Practice

There you have it: that's the DEGAP process model.

In the first part of this book, you learned about the philosophy and principles underpinning everything you'll read about in the following chapters. The remaining chapters aim to help you apply DEGAP by explaining some powerful methods for prioritizing. They offer guidance for being intentional and systematic in different (but common) generalizable scenarios.

Now, you probably won't be surprised to learn that the last phase in the DEGAP process, P, is far more involved (and in some cases much more complicated) than the preceding steps—D, E, G, and A. This is why the remaining chapters focus primarily on P. It's where things get real. Prioritization is subject to so many different variables, and you must adjust accordingly to find success. Ultimately, this book will put you in a stronger position to create better plans and make better decisions, regardless of your circumstances.

Each of the chapters that follows presents strategies, tactics, tools, and techniques for assigning items in order of importance whether you're working solo, as part of a team, or even larger organization.

The next two chapters, 8 and 9, focus on solo prioritization; in other words, prioritizing for yourself, by yourself. Then Chapters 10 and 11 shed light on how to collaborate more effectively if you are participating on or leading a team. And lastly, Chapters 12 and 13 cover prioritization in larger organizations. In concert, these chapters arm you with insights and leading indicators to help you know when your organization is doing prioritization properly...or not so much. By understanding the fundamentals of successful prioritization and training yourself to detect their presence or absence, you will be in a stronger position to apply DEGAP or to contribute to its successful application.

An important caveat: this book does not attempt to explain in detail what you need to do specifically to implement DEGAP in an organization. That would be a nearly impossible thing to do; no single trade book could hope to address the wide variety of circumstances and pressures that are unique to any single organization across the spectrum of sectors and industries. That situation would require more time and space than this short book will allow for, to say the least. Even so, you'll end up with a process and toolbox, and a much clearer idea of what's required to prioritize at an organizational scale.

3

Putting Process into Practice

If people don't understand
what the priorities are, they make
stuff up.[1]

—Lt. General Russel Honoré, US Army, Retired

1. Lt. General Russel Honoré, US Army, Retired, and Jennifer Robison, *Leadership in the New Normal*, Kindle ed. (Lafayette, LA: Acadian House Publishing, 2012).

CHAPTER

8

Personal Priorities

On June 11, 2020, as the Covid-19 pandemic was reaching its first terrifying peak in the U.S., the singer-songwriter Rosanne Cash was sitting alone on a wooden stool with her Martin OM-28 Signature Series guitar in Carnegie Hall. The lights dimmed and then the curtains opened, only to greet a crowd of no one save for a handful of sound techs and livestream operators.

At least, that's what I imagine happened. I caught a recording of the performance sometime later. As a longtime fan of Cash's and someone with a deep interest in performing at the highest levels, it had me wondering: They say that the way to Carnegie Hall is *practice, practice, practice*. But once you get there, how do you prioritize your setlist? What song do you open with, close with, and perform as an encore? What about the band arrangement? And sound setup, lighting, props, and overall production design? What outfit will you choose and what shoes (or boots) will you wear? And so on. I was super curious how people in this situation figure out their priorities.

I can only imagine the challenges of performing at a world-class venue like Carnegie Hall. So, to answer my questions, I did the obvious thing: I resolved to track down the singer, songwriter, author, artist, and eldest daughter of Johnny and Vivian Cash herself.

A little research revealed Rosanne's agent's name and contact information. In a brief email to Danny, I explained everything: the reason for my request; the topic of this book; that I was a fan of Rosanne's songs, writing, and philosophy; and that I wanted to interview somebody with first-hand experience of what it meant to play at Carnegie Hall. "Would Rosanne be open to an interview?" I asked. I hit <Send> and waited for a reply.

I was surprised to see a response from Danny less than 24 hours later. "Thank you for thinking of Rosanne for this topic. It is intriguing."

When Rosanne and I got on a Zoom call a few weeks later, I explained the idea behind the book in more detail, what I was trying to accomplish, and why I was so interested in talking with her in particular. Then I asked the million-dollar question, simple as it was: "How do you do it?" What she said struck a chord with me, to use a relevant expression.

"The number one priority? I don't want to sound New Age-y, but it's like we have to make our individual truths the priority, and out of that can come great art and deep compassion. For me, the ultimate authority is to show up for my own muse, if that doesn't sound too grand, and follow my instincts as an artist, writer, performer, and vocalist…what I'm drawn to do and what I might feel in the moment and what I want to experiment with and presenting new songs and finding balance in that. You know, to act out of it, to act out of being present, to act out of saying no to *act*. And if those instincts aren't right on, then course correct, refine, work further, and bring my discipline into it so that I can achieve that thing that I'm really reaching for."

"Beautiful. Anything else?"

"Priority number two is that as a performer, it's about connection. You know, I'm not just doing it in my living room. It's like group chemistry. And part of that is molding the energy in the room, singing to the back row, and being sensitive to what they're giving back. So, I would say that I try to take my full self on stage, respect what the audience brings, and then prioritize what is most satisfying for both of us."

She went on.

"These people are using discretionary income to come and see you and have gotten the babysitter and may have traveled far. This may be the only time they ever get to see you. Some of them are coming because they only know the top surface of your work, and you owe them the respect of doing the hits right. But I've always found I had to balance that with what I'm working on, the newest project, what I want to experiment with that really challenges me both vocally and with the band and arrangement-wise, selling-wise. So, it's a fine balance. It's respect for them and respect for myself. That starts to set the priorities for performing at Carnegie Hall."

> **HOW DOES ONE PRIORITIZE BEFORE PERFORMING AT CARNEGIE HALL?**

Rosanne Cash.

I sat quietly, slowly absorbing her perspective. It was clear that her wisdom had been gleaned from years and years of performing and life experience—much of it positive, no doubt, but some of it also challenging and unexpected. Still, despite her top-flight status, during this conversation I never felt like I was talking to anyone but a smarter, wiser friend. You don't need to be a world-renowned artist to experience the push and pull of your choices, and the trade-offs that accompany each. You just have to be human.

I also thought about what Carnegie Hall would be equivalent to for the average office employee. Was it working at Apple, Netflix, or some other high-prestige, high-stakes company? Or maybe it was executing from the C-Suite. Whatever the case, one thing was certain: anyone given an opportunity to perform in their own dream venue would be feeling the pressure. Whether it's Carnegie Hall or a potato chip factory in a nondescript suburb, the venue sets the context, conditions, and timing for our goals.

"You know, every performer is hyper-aware of the venue, especially performing at Carnegie Hall. So even added to the respect for your own instincts and respect for the audience of what they're bringing in, and the kind of group energy that you're allowing to mold and play with, there's a respect for the venue. The legacy of the venue has to be acknowledged. You can't just walk out on stage like you're walking into a bar, you know? So that in itself creates space, helps you prioritize maybe the best you have to bring."[2]

This was heavy stuff, especially coming from someone so creatively and professionally accomplished. In the wild, wooly world that's the modern music industry, surely it took a deep understanding of what to do—and, just as importantly, what not to do—to arrive at the stature Rosanne had.

So, according to Rosanne, the essence of prioritization is balancing your truth with the needs of those you serve (connecting) while paying special attention to the context in which the connection is happening.

Without paying attention—taking the time to step back and prioritize—you simply can't hope to achieve your best.

"We have to recognize that if we leave it to the unconscious, we only get so far," Rosanne explained.

2. Used with permission by Rosanne Cash.

You're the decider, whether you want to be or not; everybody else is a stakeholder. This means that whether you're prioritizing for yourself, a member of your team, or your company or organization, figuring out how to balance what's most important to you, your "audience," and your venue is what prioritizing is all about.

Choosing How You Choose

The goal of this chapter is to teach you how to become a better planner and decider by improving your ability to prioritize. It introduces some fundamental concepts when it comes to prioritizing for yourself and by yourself, all in service of successfully implementing the DEGAP process.

To help illustrate what this process looks like in the real world, I highlighted two examples of job hunting and career development from my own life. I chose these examples for two specific reasons. The first is that because they are taken from very different points in my professional life, they offer distinct perspectives on prioritization—as well as universal insights. The first story chronicles my job hunt in the heady days of 1990s Silicon Valley, while the second has me returning to my climactic moment at Rackspace, after I found out that essential members of the executive team had been fired or quit. At that point in my career, the stakes for my decision-making were a whole lot higher.

The second reason I chose these examples is that job hunting and career development offer a relatable, easy-to-understand example of what implementing DEGAP looks like.

For my money, there's not a better way to illustrate the value in deciding to prioritize prioritization than following someone at the cusp of a job search— or at the precipice of a major company transition.

That said, having a good grasp of the DEGAP process can help you in so many domains of life, not just work. While my focus here is obviously on the workplace, whether you're shopping for an e-bike, planning a vacation, or trying to create a more balanced lifestyle, following the solo prioritization playbook will get you closer to what you truly want. It's a practical, step-by-step outline for implementing the DEGAP process, empowering any individual contributor to decide wisely.

Let's begin with my own tale of early-career woe.

Making a Career Move

In the summer of 1993, roughly 20 years before my Rackspace gig, I was working at HAL Computer Systems in Campbell, California, about a 10-minute walk from where Netflix headquarters is now located. Frustrated with the politics at my job and clearly not talented enough to become a chart-topping singer-songwriter, I decided to investigate a career change. As with millions of others before and after me, this investigation inevitably led me to the book *What Color Is Your Parachute?* by Richard Nelson Bolles (the 1993 edition, to be exact).

A Practical Manual for Job Hunters & Career-Changers:

The 1993 What Color Is Your Parachute?

Richard Nelson Bolles

What Color Is Your Parachute?

I can tell you now, as I reflect back on my career, that this book changed the trajectory of my professional life. Why? It introduced me to Paired Comparison, a powerful technique for sorting a list of items that are difficult to prioritize. (My instinct that Mr. Bolles and I were on the same philosophical page turned out to be correct. Years later we became good friends, and during one of our conversations, he told me his Prioritizing Grid could be applied to just about anything.)

Inspired by the book's message, I committed to getting up a half hour early each day to work through the exercises in it. I'd start things off with a double espresso at the original Restaurante Avante on Mission Street in Santa Cruz. As I sat drinking, I'd studiously go over the book page by page. Then I'd pack up and drive the infamous Highway 17 over the Santa Cruz Mountains as I headed to the Valley for work.

People look for jobs for a host of reasons. Whether you realize it or not, these "reasons" are the result of prioritization. Unwilling to trade flexibility for higher pay? Congrats—you're prioritizing. The process of figuring out what matters to you, identifying good options, evaluating them, and then making tough trade-offs offers an object lesson in prioritization. Not to mention, one that is especially valuable when it comes to what's important both professionally and personally. Given that most of us are looking for some degree of meaning in our work, these priorities overlap quite often, as you can probably relate.

First-time job hunters seek stepping stones. Seasoned professionals in search of advancement look for new opportunities to get them closer to their goals. Someone returning to the workforce after taking time off for a sabbatical or their family may be looking for a chance to demonstrate what they're truly capable of. Whatever your intentions, the DEGAP process has something to offer.

All that being said, a quick caveat. Job hunting and career development are huge subjects that go well beyond the scope of a short book on prioritization. While the following example should help you reframe your thinking about the job search process, it's impossible for this chapter (or really, any one chapter) to give you everything you need to develop your career or guide you through a successful job hunt. (But you probably knew that.)

The Solo Prioritization Playbook: Job Hunting

If you're keen to evaluate a new opportunity, the practical application of DEGAP, which has been tweaked specifically to address the job-hunting journey, should have much to offer you. It will help you identify your potential priorities, pinpoint how to evaluate each item, and then prioritize them.

While this particular application has six steps, they all map to the larger DEGAP process. (Technically, the GAP portion of it; if you've made it to this point, you would have already completed steps D and E, having decided to engage in the prioritization process with commitment.) Here's the blueprint:

Gather

Step 1: Define the gap.

Step 2: Survey the circumstances to identify items and options.

Step 3: Clarify your values and other critical factors.

Step 4: Choose an approach.

Arrange

Step 5: Arrange items in order of importance.

Prioritize

Step 6: Evaluate and refine the results.

Gather

STEP 1: DEFINE THE GAP.

Finding a new job or developing your career requires being intellectually and emotionally honest with yourself about the reasons behind the change. You may want to work in a different location, earn a higher salary, or find an inspiring boss or fun colleagues with whom to collaborate. Some people just want a paycheck and healthcare. For others, getting paid to do what they'd do "for free" (assuming they could afford to) is the goal. All of these wants are reasonable, but just as it's important for you to accurately assess what you're looking for, it's essential to candidly assess what you're good at, as well as the trade-offs you are willing to make. These are your criteria.

As we touched on earlier, for almost everyone, job-related prioritization must take both personal and professional priorities into account. For instance, where you work may be tightly coupled to where you live (though perhaps less so in our new era of widespread remote work). And where you live may be a choice you're making because of family, friends, or personal history. And yet, where you live may need to be linked to what you do. Many highly specialized jobs exist in a particular location.

The best way to arrive at your ideal situation, (or, more realistically, ideal-enough situation) is to spell out the deeper purpose behind what's driving you. So, getting clear on your priorities matters. You can't have everything. But you can probably have most of what's really important to you. Or at least, to paraphrase the Rolling Stones, what you need. First, though, you need to understand your drivers for change.

Declare Your Outcome Drivers

Laying the foundation for any serious prioritization effort requires being completely clear on *why* something needs to change. The reasons may be self-evident or not very obvious. Regardless of how they present themselves, though, it's essential to be able to articulate them. A driver declaration can help this process along.

An outcome driver is a concise statement of the problem or opportunity that answers the question, "Why bother doing anything different?" It expresses the core motives or main reasons to leave the status quo and make a change, to move away from something less desirable and toward something better. Each outcome driver consists of three basic elements: a brief objective assertion of your current state such as, "I've been at my company for two years;" a brief description of the problem or opportunity presented such as, "I want to start my own company but lack sufficient experience;" and a value judgment that summarizes why doing something different matters—the ramifications of the change like this, "If I stick it out, I will miss some great opportunities.

Defining your outcome drivers is important. Why? Because most people are only willing to do what's necessary to change when the pain they are experiencing in the moment has become greater than the imaginary pain that they think the change will cause.

Prioritization is similar. Most people are only willing to be deliberate about the process of prioritization when the gap between their circumstances and the possibility of a better future outcome outweighs the pain they imagine (often, incorrectly) that the process of prioritizing will cause.

In my experience, one to three outcome drivers typically underpin any prioritization effort; rarely are there more than five. When there are more than one, you can list them in order of importance. Imagine, for example, that you're itching to look for a better opportunity in your field. You feel the pull to find something new and exciting and just enough of a push to leave your current job. You also acknowledge the wisdom offered by my friend Jonathan Shapiro, the CEO of Buttonsmith, that "It's easier to quit your job than to ask for it back."

Here's a fictional example rubric that illustrates how drivers work. In this case, the "problem" is potentially changing jobs. The driver here is to have a more fulfilling work experience, one that's more in line with the person's values. There are trade-offs, of course, in leaping into an entrepreneurship role willy-nilly. The person could easily fail, especially given their lack of management experience. Maybe there's a way to meet in the middle.

TABLE 8.1 HOW OUTCOME DRIVERS WORK (FICTIONAL)

CURRENT STATE	PROBLEM/ OPPORTUNITY	RAMIFICATIONS
I've been at my current company for two years. My boss has the job I want, but he'll probably never leave, and he reports directly to our founder/CEO. I don't know what it takes to manage managers, multiple products, and a large budget.	Entrepreneurship runs deep in my family. I already know that I eventually want to start my own company. But I lack the experience of being an operational leader in an executive role.	If I stick it out in hopes of getting promoted, I will probably miss some great opportunities. But jumping into my own thing too early could lead to a preventable failure and a bad outcome.

Perhaps this person could go work at a small but growing startup, where they'd probably advance quickly through the ranks while getting more management experience under their belt. The important thing is that they know what is motivating them. So instead of working toward an abstract indicator of "success" (a particular job title, for example), they are empowered to progress in a way that satisfies their own personal driver(s). This will ultimately steer them in the right path, even if it's not quite what they expected and they have to face down several setbacks.

Outcome drivers link undesirable circumstances to actionable change. They gesture toward a possible vision and connect it to the desired outcome. Find your driver for change, find your (workplace) liberation.

Here's a real-life example of someone beginning to think through how they can progress from their current state to a more desirable one, drawn from one of my executive coaching clients:

TABLE 8.2 HOW OUTCOME DRIVERS WORK
(REAL-LIFE EXAMPLE)

CURRENT STATE	PROBLEM/ OPPORTUNITY	RAMIFICATIONS
I'm not sure whether my boss will promote me or fire me. He's terrible at giving useful feedback. I am a senior director. I'm working harder than ever. But the fires start first thing in the morning, and by the end of the day I'm exhausted but haven't worked on the things that move the needle.	I feel like I am running up a down escalator. I want to be a difference-maker. I want to know that I am competent and well respected. I want some sense of job security.	There's a real possibility I'm going to fail and lose my job.

Here's the version that my client crafted into an outcome driver to spell out her compelling reason for change:

> Honestly, I'm not sure whether my boss will promote me or fire me. Now that I am finally a senior director, I'm working harder than I ever have but feel like I am running up a down escalator. The fires start first thing in the morning, and by the end of the day I'm exhausted but haven't worked on the things that will move the needle. This sucks because I want to be a difference-maker. I want to know that I am competent and well respected. I certainly don't want to get canned. I need a new gig.

The takeaway is that when you're crystal clear about what's propelling a change, the rest of the process will unfold more intuitively. Outcome drivers help establish the "as-is" conditions of your gap. Your desired outcomes define the future, a "to-be" picture of possibilities.

Unlock Your Desired Outcome

The Desired Outcome model, first mentioned in Chapter 5, spells out the all the details of a desirable outcome. It helps people envision the size and scope of the gap between the current state and desired state. This is key. Without this information, you won't know what success actually looks like.

You need to know upfront what evidence will indicate that you're on track. Establishing this will help bridge the gap, increasing the likelihood that your efforts will yield more of what you want and less of what you don't. On that note, take a moment to answer the first two questions of the Desired Outcome model: What do you want?

- **What's the higher-order outcome?**

If you use the example from the rubric earlier, about looking for a new work opportunity, here's what the answers might look like:

- **What do you want?** A great new job.

- **What's the higher-order outcome?** The confidence that I'm on the right career path.

When you get to question #3 of the Desired Outcome model, "What is the evidence for success?" stop and reflect on how you'll know you have what you want. What will the evidence of success be? It's one thing to say, "I'll have a great job." It's another entirely to say, "A job where I earn $110k a year, have an opportunity for advancement, and I'm learning about all aspects of my industry." The first statement offers "evidence" that is too vague to be meaningful.

Don't forget to check in with yourself during this process; doing so will go a long way in helping you uncover your needs, interests, and goals. Consider consulting your inner pragmatist, who will tell you the truth about what success might *actually* look like. (Spoiler alert: It may not be what you originally envisioned!) But don't let reality hinder your dreams. Accepting it can be a powerful way to shed light on what matters and why.

STEP 2: SURVEY THE CIRCUMSTANCES TO IDENTIFY ITEMS AND OPTIONS.

When it comes to job hunting, there are two diametrically opposed philosophies:

- Do what you love, and the money will follow.

- Do what you're good at and the love will follow (then the money…hopefully).

Regardless of which philosophy you subscribe to, finding a gig that inspires and excites you or one that you're naturally good at requires you to be deliberate about your process. This means identifying items, arranging them in order of importance, and highlighting the ones to pursue based on your criteria and priorities. Along the way you'll need to do your research. You'll need to talk to stakeholders—spouse, partners, family—people who might be impacted by your shifting priorities. And you'll need to perform due diligence that will greatly impact your decision- and priority-making.

STEP 3: CLARIFY YOUR VALUES AND OTHER CRITICAL FACTORS.

Your values are what's most important to you. Whether you are conscious of them or not, these deep-seated esteemed beliefs and attitudes will nudge your decisions, words, and actions in accordance with them. Values are not just what you say they are; rather, they are what you do in practice. In fact, many would argue the latter (your behavior) is a much greater indication of your values than the former (your words).

Note that a value is not simply a broad focus area such as "family," "health," "career," or "community." In contrast, values express your truest feelings, beliefs, and overarching orientation. Contrast the previous list with this one: "spending quality time with my family," "keeping my body strong and resilient," "growing my career," or "serving my community." All of these are far better expressions of values. While other elements of your lives such as commitments, dependencies, and existential questions can alter your course of action, they typically don't motivate you as much as your values do. Not willingly, at least.

When it comes to a job search or career change, it is wise to make the mental space for figuring out what is truly most and least important to you. Not only will this help you make better decisions and ones that you're unlikely to have to undo later on, but it will also put you in a position to consider the values of a company or organization you're thinking about joining, and whether there's a match or mismatch between yours and theirs. If you want to be "a valued member of a winning team on an inspiring mission,"[3] as the Rackspace job ad put it, but they're willing to pay top dollar to be a warm butt in an empty seat in a soulless machine, you better make sure you're all about the money. If not, you should probably look somewhere else for that new gig.

---

3. "Leading Through Constant and Unpredictable Change," *Founders Series* (blog), August 11, 2020, www.rackspace.com/solve/leading-through-constant-and-unpredictable-change

Prioritizing Assumptions

Fair or not, your assumptions influence your decision-making in small or big ways—just as they do for everyone. But assumptions aren't necessarily true; they are uncritically held beliefs you hold about reality. They silently shape how you see and engage the world around you. As a result, it's important to pressure test any assumption that could, were it to later turn out to be inaccurate, cause a critical decision not to stand up.

For instance, I assume some people are interested in what I say. I also believe that people are keenly interested in the topic of prioritization. And I think that people will buy this book. Prioritizing my assumptions means rearranging the list below in order of importance, from top to bottom. I assume that:

- Businesses will buy this book for their employees.

- Ambitious people are interested in the topic of prioritization.

- People who are interested in professional growth are curious about what I have to say.

How could I test these assumptions? A few ways. One is through beta reading: giving a (reasonably polished) draft of the book manuscript to people in my target audience to review. If their feedback is generally positive, then it suggests, though doesn't wholly confirm, I'm onto something. If it's negative or lukewarm, it may mean that I picked the wrong audience; my idea isn't as great as I thought; or my idea is good, but my writing needs more work. Either way, this is information I can use as I decide how to proceed with the book.

Another way is to get in touch with business colleagues and casually gauge their interest in a book on prioritization. In a way I've already done this, though in a backward fashion: this book came about precisely because so many people in my work orbit were asking me to write about prioritization. This is a useful starting point to proceed from, since it strongly suggests there's some demand for the book.

In summary, identifying and prioritizing assumptions allows you to pinpoint what you need to pay attention to and then test the degree to which they are (or are not) in fact true.

An ability to identify assumptions and clarify what's most important to you (your values) is often the key to making successful career choices.

Prioritizing Commitments, Constraints, or Dependencies

Commitments, constraints, and dependencies are quite different from values and assumptions. Instead of guiding choices *toward* a result, they limit your options and outcomes.

Commitments link you to the agreements you have made or contracts you have signed and come in two forms, hard and soft. Typically, hard commitments are ones that have some kind of contractual relationship. For instance, if you signed a noncompete agreement with a former employer, there's a chance that joining a competitor could trigger a nastygram or perhaps some sort of legal action.

On the other hand, soft commitments are generally nonbinding, at least in a legal sense. Ignore them, however, at your own peril. Giving them short shrift may damage your reputation if people perceive that you did not do what you said or implied. Some refer to this as your say-do ratio: the link between what you commit to (your words) and whether you follow through (your actions). For instance, several years ago I declared I was going to write this book. For the subsequent years that I was toiling away, struggling to get these ideas out of my head and onto "paper," certain members of my family and many of my closest friends expressed concern about my say-do ratio. And for good reason!

As far as it relates to job hunting and career development, constraints are critical limiting factors. Minimum salary, location, hours, etc. are usually the first things job seekers look at when they're evaluating a prospective opportunity. Constraints can often be quantified with numbers and data. For example, today, the annual household income required for a family of four to live above the poverty line in the San Francisco Bay Area is about $150k. Therefore, taking a job at a really cool nonprofit for $85k a year might be a great idea. Or it might be a terrible one, depending on one's circumstances.

Finally, dependencies can include anything on which a follow-up item relies. For instance, getting a great job as a privacy professional typically requires a Certified Information Privacy Professional (CIPP) credential. This tells the company that you know privacy laws and regulations and how to apply them. It means that you have a foundational understanding of broad global concepts of privacy and data protection law and practice.

Identifying dependencies is key because if one of your potential priorities involves an output that other people need to consume, you will probably need to elevate its priority. The more people there are who depend on a decision you make (or don't), the greater the consequences of that decision.

Prioritizing Open Questions

The final part of clarifying your values and other critical factors is to ask the right questions about the who, what, why, when, and how.

This is easier said than done. "We rarely ask ourselves or others the right questions,"[4] writes Matthew Fray in *This Is How Your Marriage Ends*, the bestselling meditation on relationships both personal and otherwise. "What are the right questions? The right questions challenge your assumptions and beliefs and force us to consider an alternative," he explains.[5] I'd add that the quality of your questions will determine the impact of the answers. This is critical, since, as Fray says, high-quality answers can provide profoundly valuable insights about the choices in front of you, which may have long-term positive or negative consequences, many perhaps unintended.

This means you should take the time to allow the most important questions to percolate into your prioritization process. The way to do this? Identify questions that are specific, insightful, and penetrating. Rank them in order of importance. And then answer them in that order.

Introducing Stack Ranking

Speaking of ranking, let's take a quick detour to go over a more formal approach to it called *Stack Ranking*. This is the most basic qualitative way to prioritize anything, and it can be a handy tool for making your way through the DEGAP process. Stack Ranking is often the simplest way to prioritize a small set of items (fewer than 25, in my experience).

To start, create a list of the items to be prioritized. Evaluate them and then rearrange them from highest to lowest priority, or vice-versa. You can label them with numbers or letters or jot them down and rearrange them on a computer, whiteboard, or piece of paper. Whatever works best. I often use Post-it notes on a table at a coffee shop.

4. Matthew Fray, *This Is How Your Marriage Ends: A Hopeful Approach to Saving Relationships*, read by Rob Shapiro (Harper Audio 2022), Audible audiobook; unabr., 9 hrs., 15 min.
5. Matthew Fray, "Is Your Spouse Hurting You on Purpose?" *The Good Men Project* (blog), May 13, 2016, www.goodmenproject.com/featured-content/is-your-spouse-hurting-you-on-purposematthewfray-jrmk

The idea is to evaluate your list based on explicit criteria like benefit or value. Or you can rank your list based on implicit factors, arrange them as you see fit, and then determine what was behind your choices. Move what feels like the most important item to the top, the least important item to the bottom, and then rearrange the ones in the middle according to their relative importance or value. Iterate until it feels right.

Not Stack-Ranked   Stack-Ranked

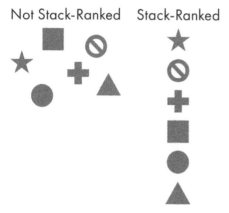

Stack Ranking example.

People sometimes refer to this approach as *force ranking* because at first items may seem to be of equal value, but the rules "force" you to make tough choices. Items can't be equal in a stack-ranked list, so you must choose which is more or less valuable to you. However, the order of the items needn't necessarily dictate the decisions you make or actions you take. Rather, the list informs the options you have, and the order helps you see how items "stack" up against each other. Just because you've designated something the "most important" does not necessarily mean that it should must be tackled immediately.

Stack Ranking is fairly straightforward when you're doing it by yourself. But it can get tricky in a group setting.[6] And the process can get sticky if items are too similar, the criteria for choosing among them are in conflict, or when items are in competing categories. Remember Fredkin's Paradox? The more similar options are, the more difficult it will be and the longer it will take to choose among them. That said, when two or more items end up competing for the same logical level, there is a clever work-around for breaking the tie.

---

6. Sunni Brown, *The Doodle Revolution*, ill. ed. (New York, NY: Portfolio/Penguin 2015).

The trick is to extract the underlying reasons that one is more or less important before you choose. You can do this by arbitrarily placing one item over the other and then asking these questions: If you had to choose, with no way out, which would it be? Why—what was the underlying reason? Figuring this out almost always makes it easier to break a tie.

STEP 4: CHOOSE AN APPROACH.

This is where the rubber meets the road. Choosing your approach involves identifying the criteria you'll use and selecting the method(s) for actually prioritizing your options. For solo prioritization, how do you know whether to use a framework or a sorting technique? I may sound like a broken record, but *it depends*. If time permits, start with a suitable framework, and then follow it with a sorting technique to help you simplify and clarify your understanding of the options before you.

If you're stumped, choose the Eisenhower Matrix to call attention to what's urgent and important. See if the Fast vs. Right framework (see the Appendix) can help you "guesstimate" how quickly you need to act versus how rigorous you need to be. Or employ Stack Ranking or Paired Comparison sorting techniques (also just below) to force you to make even the most difficult call.

After you decide on a framework or a sorting technique, you'll be in a stronger position to begin prioritizing your items.

Remember, just because the end result of your prioritization is an ordered list, you will still have the prerogative to make choices about what, ultimately, is most important. As ever, you are the decider.

Paired Comparison

As it turns out, the secret ingredient in *What Color Is Your Parachute?* is a sorting technique that the author, Richard Bolles, called *pairwise comparison*. I refer to this method as *Paired Comparison*. This general-purpose sorting technique prompts you to identify, evaluate, and prioritize just about anything.

Here's how it works. Paired Comparison lets you score a list of items after you've compared each item against the others. In each pair, you judge which of each item is more important to you. It's essentially an iterative process where items compete head-to-head (one-on-one) in a duel. Each item gets a point for a one-on-one win.

The simplest application of Paired Comparison doesn't allow ties. So, you have to decide which item you prefer within a pair. In the end, the item with the highest number of total points is Priority 1. The item with the next-highest number is Priority 2, and so on.

STEP 1	STEP 2	STEP 3	STEP 4	STEP 5
Items	Comparison	Raw Score	Tie Breaker	Prioritized

STEP 1 Items	STEP 3 Raw Score	STEP 4 Tie Breaker	STEP 5 Prioritized
A. Spaghetti	A. Spaghetti 5	A. Spaghetti 5	1. Pancakes
B. Ravioli	B. Ravioli 3	B. Ravioli 3	2. Spaghetti
C. Pancakes	C. Pancakes 6	C. Pancakes 6	3. Ravioli
D. Sushi	D. Sushi 0	D. Sushi 0	4. Ice cream
E. Salmon	E. Salmon 1	E. Salmon 1	5. Choc cake
F. Ice cream	F. Ice cream 3	F. Ice cream 3	6. Salmon
G. Choc cake	G. Choc cake 3	G. Choc cake 3	7. Sushi

Paired Comparison example.

Paired Comparison is an excellent tool for prioritizing what matters in a job opportunity. In this situation, each item would be a different work requirement you have or aspect of a job that's on offer. Let's look at the example below to see why a Paired Comparison can work so well.

Imagine that you're ready to change jobs. As part of the process, you start thinking about the sorts of places you'll apply to and their requirements. One of them is workplace location. Will the job allow you to work from home, in a remote office, part-time in a hybrid setup, or will you be required to be in the office full-time? Being the master of prioritization that you are, you realize that you need to figure out where you stand on this issue before you start applying.

Here's what your list of items might look like:

- Work from home (WFH)
- Remote office
- Hybrid (WFH and corporate HQ)
- Corporate HQ

To execute the Paired Comparison, start by comparing A with B, then A with C, and then A with D. Ask yourself, "What's more important, A or B?" Let's say *WFH* wins, so put a check mark by A. Next, compare A to C. Let's say *hybrid* wins, so put another check by C. Then compare A with D. Let's say *WFH* wins again. At this point, A has two check marks and C has one.

Next, compare B with C, and B with D. Ask yourself, "What's more important, B or C?" In this case, *hybrid* wins, so put a check mark by C. Next, compare B to D. Say you prefer D, corporate HQ; put a check by D. At this point, you have two votes for A, no votes for B, three votes for C, and one vote for D.

Go on to compare C with D. Ask yourself, yet again, "What's more important? C (a hybrid working environment) or D (having to show up at HQ every day)?"

The bottom line is that this is a permutation comparison of each item to all other items.

Arrange

STEP 5: ARRANGE ITEMS IN ORDER OF IMPORTANCE.

For purposes of this experiment, let's restart the process with the understanding that you prefer working in a hybrid fashion. You like the freedom of working from home but also enjoy visiting the office to meet with your teammates and socialize on occasions, so you put a check mark by C every time it's a contender.

When you finish comparing each item with every other item, you tally the votes or check marks. The item with the most votes moves to the top spot, while the item with the second largest number of votes moves to position #2, and so on and so forth.

Here's how the list could look:

1. Hybrid (WFH and corporate HQ)
2. Work from home (WFH)
3. Corporate headquarters
4. Remote office

Excellent. You've ranked an essential set of criteria.

As you arrange your various items in order of importance, your priorities will inevitably begin to settle. In my experience, simply going through the process can surface what's most important and make previously tacit criteria become explicit and self-evident. At this point, according to Troy Toman, VP of Software Engineering at Planet, prioritizing is "more of an act of declaration."[7] It's something you already know but are now giving voice to and saying out loud.

The secret of this process is its simplicity. Paired Comparison is good for cajoling you to make a series of simple, binary choices that add up to a list of items that you have stack ranked in order of importance, top-to-bottom. It's particularly good for sorting lists of items that aren't too long (say, 25 or fewer), where items are somewhat similar (or at least in the same general category), and when you haven't yet defined the criteria to compare and contrast the items against.

One caveat: Paired Comparison isn't the most efficient technique to use if items are changing or additional ones are constantly being added. This is because you compare each item in the raw list against the others. If the list is stable, you can go through it just once. If things change, you need to run through the entire list again.

If circumstances are more dynamic or complex than anticipated, you can turn to more sophisticated prioritization tools such as Simple Weighted Scoring, a matrix (spreadsheet) that utilizes weighted criteria. But that's a bit much for this chapter—more on that in Chapter 10.

Prioritize

STEP 6: EVALUATE AND REFINE THE RESULTS.
Regardless of the approach you ultimately use to prioritize, you will probably find it helpful, if not essential, to share the results of your efforts with key stakeholders. Since this is solo prioritization, your key stakeholders are people who will be affected, but not likely to be part of the prioritization process, beyond contributing input and perhaps providing info during the Gather phase of DEGAP.

They can provide a valuable extra set of eyes to help identify what you might have missed. And it's far easier to reprioritize a list of potential items than undo a set of decisions once you've put those priorities into action.

---

7. Used with permission by Troy Toman.

When you're okay with your results, and you can see, with deep insight, how your options stack up against one another, you are done (for the moment, at least). You'll have a clear line of sight in terms of your options and why each of them is important, or less important, in their own way.

Ultimately, my job search led me to work at Apple Computer in the networking group on Bandley Drive in Cupertino. And, since my exodus from HAL Computer Systems, I've worked with other companies, big and small. Hot new things and legacy corporations. Through it all, there have been sweet victories and crushing failures. The end result, however, is that I've gained an intuitive understanding of the art and science behind weighing competing demands.

Rackspace: Prioritize or Die Trying

Back to that fateful day at Rackspace in 2014. As I mentioned in Chapter 1, after I got that unexpected call from my coworker Gigi, the VP of Engineering at Rackspace, I sat in a Tacoma hotel eating my bagel and reflecting on the fact that I was responsible for managing priorities that affected some 1,000 Rackers (employees) and, by extension, potentially millions of customers.

I immediately returned to the Castle (Rackspace HQ) to size up the situation. With our CEO, president, and SVP of Product out, I was on a fact-finding mission of one. Should I stay or should I go? And if I chose the former, how was I going to approach the challenge?

A deluge of emails, voicemails, and requests by frontline managers desperate to discuss the situation greeted me upon my return. The individual contributors who reported to them (and some of the managers themselves) were rightfully concerned about how the leadership changes would affect them. They were worried about their jobs, and they wanted advice. If they, and the company, were going to successfully work through this major restructuring, important decisions would have to be made. And the right priorities would have to be sussed out. Helping employees do both was my primary new role.

Although I didn't realize it at the time, my thought process was similar in so many ways to Rosanne's as she prepared to perform in places like Carnegie Hall. First and foremost, I had to show up for my own muse. I had to figure out that what was important to me was sticking it out and doing what

I could to ease the leadership transition for the Rackers who remained as I stepped back into the situation at Rackspace.

Next, I had to figure out what was needed in the current context of major upheaval. I also had to understand the needs of my "audience": the SLT (the senior leadership team), now in transition; line management; my own team; and 1,000 plus employees who still remained in our org.

Like Rosanne, I had to play, in effect, to the people in the back of the room.

And finally, I had to respect the venue. Rackspace was an amazing place. It had an astonishingly quirky culture. (It was housed in a converted shopping mall, for God's sake!) To paraphrase Rosanne, I couldn't show up to HQ, which at the time was gripped by anxiety over the company's future, like I was walking into a bar.

After I committed myself to staying, once again, I immediately began applying the DEGAP process to reevaluate our business unit's priorities, although I didn't yet call DEGAP by its current acronym. (At this point in my career I hadn't yet formalized the system. I was more or less operating at the level of unconscious competence. It would be a few more years until I spelled out my process in written detail, and still more until I incorporated it into a book.)

The results, I think, speak for themselves. After weighing several very strong item candidates, Rackspace product leadership ultimately decided that prioritizing user-interface design improvements for our OpenStack private cloud offering would give us the most bang for our collective buck. The framework I used to help accomplish the transition was the Max Priorities Pyramid. See Chapter 12 for more information on setting priorities at scale.

Under our former leadership team, the company had been spread somewhat thin, and we thought focusing on our private cloud offerings—a serious growth opportunity for us—would bring our various teams in alignment and provide a quick victory that could boost morale and reassure everyone that the ship was righting.

Less than a year later, the private cloud had become a central pillar of our strategy. After completing this project, I went on to develop new customer experience capabilities within a half-dozen cross-functional teams inside the company. These were important achievements. And they all started with me taking time out to assess what truly needed to be done—first by myself, and then by my team(s).

An executive role like the one I was in at Rackspace is, in effect, a performance. You're not making music, true, nor are you depicting a character from a novel. But you are playing a role. Any senior leadership position requires that you perform, in the sense that you must evaluate your venue, play to your audience, and decide what actions you are going to take (and, just as importantly, not take) to make meaning for them.

I still recall the flight attendant speech just before taking off from Tacoma and heading back to Texas. It's the one you've heard a million times and undoubtedly tune out every time you fly: the one where you're instructed to secure your own mask first before helping others.

Sitting on the tarmac that afternoon, waiting to fly home to a huge, quickly growing mess, I found myself paying attention to the speech for some reason. I guess it spoke to me at the moment. It reminded me that if I was going to show up fully prepared for the challenges at Rackspace and with my team and larger organization, the first thing I was going to need to do was get my own priorities in order. Once I did that, I could take a step back and look at the needs and priorities of the teams I was leading.

After I decided what I needed to do, slowly but surely, the other pieces began to fall into place. Figuring out what matters most is the surest way to a stellar performance.

When you finish prioritizing, you can move forward with confidence and begin exploring new opportunities. Hopefully, this will put you in a better position to deliver on existing commitments, renegotiate ones that you now feel aren't as important, and make new commitments with more confidence. You should be in a stronger position to evaluate with your head and your heart and to continue your quest for a new gig, job, or career move. This, in turn, will give you more confidence to take bold action when it comes to making those tough trade-offs. That's what's in it for you.

That's the good news. The tougher pill to swallow: nearly anybody can prioritize a set of projects, problems, opportunities, or actions once. But turning prioritization into a habitual practice requires a repeatable system and workflow, a process that ensures you're consistently acting on what matters most and leaving distractions behind.

9

Prioritizing for Yourself Periodically

Most people tend to do work as it shows up. It's understandable: Someone sends you an email with a request that they insist or imply is urgent, your stress level spikes, and you feel an impulse to respond immediately. Tackling something *right now* just seems like the best option at the moment.

The problem here is twofold. The first is that over the course of any given day, the requests inevitably pile up and up and up—big, small, and medium requests, all of them supposedly urgent. The second is that the kind of work that most people are being asked to do rarely *starts out* well-planned or well-defined enough for you to complete it competently without refinement.

Reacting to events as they unfold is the behavior of someone who has lost control of the timeline. It's a common byproduct of someone who lacks a reliable system for identifying (and refreshing) what they need to stay focused on.

It's the habit of someone who probably finds it challenging to manage all their commitments (especially to themself) and make constant progress on longer-term goals.

Being reactive, rather than proactive and intentional, is the behavior of someone whose gap between their present state and desired future state is at constant risk of expanding, maybe beyond repair. To be sure, sometimes losing control of the timeline is unavoidable. However, it's most often a byproduct of not properly identifying, selecting, and executing top priorities. It's the result of not prioritizing prioritization, especially when it's emotionally demanding or difficult to do.

For purposes of our discussion, let's call this kind of unplanned and often undefined work, "interrupts." If left unchecked, interrupts rip your attention away from what you've predetermined is most important and make it harder to get back to work. This is especially true if you haven't invested the time and energy to define the work that needs to be done and then prioritized it.

To shift your focus away from being *more efficient* to being *more effective*, you can prioritize periodically. This means quarterly, weekly, or daily—whatever time intervals are appropriate given your circumstances. Doing so will help you maintain a more fluid set of potential priorities to choose from, ultimately putting you in a stronger position to rearrange your top priorities and put other items on the backburner. It lets you dig into the right work—or dive back into it if you get distracted or interrupted, as you inevitably will. (Even the most battle-hardened practitioners of prioritization [me included] occasionally struggle to resist the siren call of the urgent.)

The main reason that people don't prioritize regularly is that they mistakenly think it's hard to do. They conflate prioritizing with having a robust system for getting things done or perfectly managing their time. But that's not the case. Prioritizing regularly is a distinctly separate act, and one that's easy to implement in your daily life.

Develop the DEGAP Habit

Most people confuse the process of periodic prioritization with personal productivity. But there's a subtle and important difference between the two. For one, successful periodic prioritization requires turning DEGAP into a habit. This means it becomes an automatic process for quickly deciding, engaging, gathering, arranging, and prioritizing a relatively small number of extremely important items, regardless of what they are and regardless of whether they will accelerate your ability to get stuff done. The focus of the DEGAP habit is efficacy—creating better plans, making smarter decisions, and taking more effective action.

Personal productivity, on the other hand, emphasizes being able to accomplish more over a shorter period of time, in other words, efficiency. The main focus is on increasing your velocity. There's no doubt that learning how to speed up your ability to get sh*t done can be profoundly useful. But the question is, "should you focus on this or that" vs. "how can you do more, faster?" If your priorities are off-kilter, then being more productive just means you'll dig yourself into a deeper hole that much faster. The last thing you want is to be fooled into thinking you know "exactly what you need to do" and be flat wrong. It happens all too often when solo prioritization hasn't taken place.

Arguably the most popular system for personal productivity today is described in the bestselling book, *Getting Things Done: The Art of Stress-Free Productivity* by David Allen, the world's best-known productivity guru. Commonly shortened to GTD®, Allen's methodology for getting things done provides a system and workflow for keeping your head clear of unnecessary details.

Allen's method also offers GTD practitioners a set of specific actions and responses for dealing with the constant interrupts, surprises, and new information they face every day, empowering GTD practitioners to slice effortlessly through the jungle of their day with a mental machete.

Allen attempts to solve for the fact that when you try to keep track of obligations in your heads, you create "open loops," which make you anxious. That anxiety, in turn, reduces your ability to think effectively. If you could avoid worrying about what you were supposed to be doing, you could focus more fully on what you were actually doing. To that end, the essence of the GTD methodology focuses on capturing and processing "inputs" by triaging them, pinpointing action steps to resolve them, and executing these steps.

Most solo prioritization and personal productivity systems—and GTD is no exception—have some overlap. Many ask you to capture and clarify all of the items that might need your attention, pinpoint what's both urgent and important, and then actively work on what matters most. This approach attempts to limit the amount of work in progress (WIP) at any given moment by queuing in a backlog[1] whatever you're not presently focused on at the moment. This approach gives you the option, should you so choose, to address other items later on. So, to a limited extent, GTD does speak to prioritization.

But this is where the similarities mostly end. Being really good at maximizing your productivity can only take you so far. Again, there's not much point in accomplishing a lot if you're accomplishing the wrong stuff or not enough of the right stuff. To put it in slightly cheekier terms, you can think of productivity as Mr. Right Now, and prioritizing as Mr. Right.

Do You Need an Upgrade?

Obviously, most professionals can benefit from improving their productivity. I know I certainly can. But having an ongoing prioritization practice is, in my opinion, much more useful for getting you closer toward your goals—aka closing that gap.

If you're still not sure if you're ripe for developing a regular practice, you can use the following quick test. Ask yourself these four telling questions:

- Do you know exactly what your top priorities are every day?
- Do you focus on what's truly urgent and most important, even when it's tough?
- Is what you need to focus on crisply defined and clearly actionable?
- If you're interrupted or distracted, do you refocus and get back to your priorities?

If you answer *yes* (at least most of the time) to all of them, congratulations. You have conquered one of modern life's greatest challenges—staying focused on what matters most. Feel free to ignore the rest of this chapter and introduce it to somebody else who may need it more.

If, however, you answered *no, sort of,* or *I don't know* to any of them, or if you feel overwhelmed, or have a vague sense that you're not focused on the right things, then consider the possibility you need to upgrade your approach. Put simply,

---

1. A note for people who are unfamiliar with Agile software development methodology: the word *backlog* may make it sound like you're already behind. But that's not necessarily the case. Backlogs can include items of all shapes and sizes that might or might not have previously been prioritized or well-formed but need to be cataloged for potential future consideration.

when you have a system for selecting and choosing where to focus (and refocus) your attention, it will be much easier to pull what's most important into the foreground and push what's less important onto the back burner. As a result, some things won't get done or won't get done promptly. If you're asking yourself, "But what about the messages I'm ignoring and getting to Inbox Zero?[2]"

Without a doubt, better prioritization will help tremendously. Empowering you to focus on what's most critical will allow you to defer or ignore what's relatively less important. Please understand that effective prioritization alone won't solve all your personal productivity challenges. That's beyond the scope of this book. Priorities are about putting you in a stronger position to say "no" to what's important so you can say "yes" to what's *most* important. That's what having a system for selecting and choosing where to focus your attention is all about.

Moreover, once you have an established system in place, any new items that present themselves can simply be slotted in and put through the decision-making sausage grinder with minimal drama. An undeniable fact is this: It's not easy to be successful on a team or in an organization unless you can prioritize for yourself repeatedly, day in and day out.

So, if you're jumping into a new professional environment, and especially if you're taking on a new role with additional responsibilities, getting an upgrade in the form of a DEGAP habit is a sure-fire way to improve your chances of making a good impression and bridging whatever gaps lie before you.

Mastering Your Morning

One simple but powerful way to habituate yourself to prioritizing is with the Morning Boot Routine.[3] It's an easy, effective way of applying the core principles of DEGAP, and it can benefit almost anyone. Think of it as *DEGAP Lite*.

Apart from helping you clarify what really counts, this process will familiarize you with the DEGAP philosophy, loosening up your prioritization muscles for when you decide you're ready to fully implement DEGAP.

---

2. Merlin Mann, "Inbox Zero," *Google TechTalks* (podcast), July 23, 2007, www.youtu.be/z9UjeTMb3Yk?si=KWvCKUC3DTDuwC-a
3. In this context, *boot* refers to the act of starting or booting up a complex system like a computer, not footwear. I think of each day as a complex system of conversations, commitments, decisions, and actions. As a result, the Morning Boot Routine starts up the day.

The aim of this exercise is to quickly give some traction to your prioritization efforts, i.e., it can help you do the following:

- Identify and tackle what you are avoiding.
- Pinpoint what's most time-sensitive.
- Highlight the next step toward your North Star (top long-term) goal.

The Morning Boot Routine is a straightforward, daily thing you do. Routines prompt people to get good at repeating activities they might otherwise let slide, but you need to do it regularly to derive long-term benefits. And if you do it day in and day out, it becomes automatic.

Morning Boot Routine.

Quick Start: The Morning Boot Routine

Assuming that you've carved out 15 minutes or so, you'll need to run through the process and find a place where you won't be interrupted. Once you've done that, it's time to get started.

STEP 1: MAKE A LIST OF EVERYTHING ON YOUR PLATE.

To ensure that nothing falls through the cracks, write down all of the following in a list format: to-dos, tasks you need to start, projects you need to make progress on, jobs that need to be done, and final details you need to tie on to things you've just about completed. In my experience (and according to science[4]), paper works best, since it requires more deliberate effort, but feel free to use your phone, tablet, or computer if they're easier for you.

Next, note any deadlines that are looming, outstanding commitments, problems you're facing, opportunities on the horizon, and especially important long-term goals you want to achieve.

There's a method to the madness of this purge. "Getting everything out of your head is the single best thing you can do" to gain perspective, writes Stanford University design instructor Christina Wodtke.[5] So, go ahead and purge away.

STEP 2: IDENTIFY YOUR AVOIDANCES, TIME-SENSITIVE ITEMS, AND STRATEGIC NEXT STEPS.

Wrack your brain to identify what you're avoiding, willfully ignoring, or procrastinating on. Be painfully honest with yourself. You don't need to share this list with anybody else—it's for you alone, as sacrosanct as a journal or a diary. Scott Sehlhorst, President of Tyner Blain, Inc., says, "I really think this is a secret weapon. The few times I've done it, it has really been special. Like the Pomodoro technique of prioritization. Difficult, and worth it."

Nobody likes to think about what they're avoiding, but there's a good chance that once you acknowledge it and eventually deal with it, you'll feel a sense of relief and have a renewed infusion of energy. Dealing with it or accepting that nothing can be done and moving on, is a surefire way to release pent-up energy that can be directed productively toward other things you want to achieve, and which may bring you more joy.

The simplest way to tag what you're avoiding is to put an "A" next to it. Identifying and working on your avoidances is the single most important

---

4. Cindi May, "A Learning Secret: Don't Take Notes with a Laptop," *Scientific American*, June 3, 2014, www.scientificamerican.com/article/a-learning-secret-don-t-take-notes-with-a-laptop

5. Christina Wodtke, *Radical Focus: Achieving Your Most Important Goals with Objectives and Key Results*, 2nd ed. (Palo Alto, CA: self-pub., Cucina Media, LLC, 2021).

concept in this book. If you take away nothing else from reading this book, don't ignore this. It's *the* difference that makes the difference.

Next, identify items that are truly time sensitive. These are the kinds of items that have a high cost of delay, such that if you don't address them promptly, they might cause you to pay a price for waiting or even lose control of a timeline. As a result, you'll be forced to react to them when and if they pop back up, causing your stress level to go up substantially. Buying airline tickets are my favorite example. The longer you wait, the more expensive they become. And, eventually, all the seats will be sold out. I suggest putting a "T" next to those items. Finally, identify the items that will help you make progress toward longer-term (but no less important) strategic or North Star goals. You can put a "G" to the left of them.

Now review your list. If it's obvious what you will need to do to make progress on an item, take a moment to reflect on it. If not, reword the item in a way that makes it abundantly clear what you would actually need to do to make progress. Remove any ambiguity or vagueness. If the item is too big, break it down into smaller chunks (i.e., several list items) until the details are obvious and can be acted on concretely.

STEP 3: RANK YOUR AVOIDANCES, TIME-SENSITIVE ITEMS, AND NEXT STEPS.

If you see more than one item with an "A," stack rank or use Paired Comparison to rank the list from most-to-least important. Write "1," next to your biggest avoidance (e.g., the item with an A that's ranked as most important).

Do the same thing for items with a "T" next to them. Sort them by Cost of Delay; the higher the cost, the higher they belong in your list. Then write "2" next to the item that's most urgent or pressing.

Now repeat this process one more time, identifying the item whose completion is most essential for making progress on your North Star goal. Pay particular attention to people who are waiting or depending on you. And increase the ranking of an action step that unblocks *someone else* from making progress on your goal.[6] Mark this item with a "3."

6. Dan Charnas, *Work Clean: The Life-Changing Power of Mise-en-Place to Organize Your Life, Work, and Mind,* read by Dan Charnas (Random House Audio, 2016), Audible audiobook, unabr., 8 hr., 50 min.

After you've done these rankings, pressure-test your list. Be brutally honest with yourself. Do these three items actually reflect your three most important priorities? Does the list make logical sense? Does it feel intuitively correct?

In *First Things First*, Stephen Covey suggests that when it's time to make a decision, you should "consult the wisdom of your heart as well as your mind."[7] If your rankings don't align with your heart and mind, great, ask yourself the question I return to time and time again in the 21st Century Leadership training I attended in Tacoma, Washington, in 2014: "What am I pretending not to know?"

Although the items in your list may obviously require more time than just a day to complete, start by picking the item that's most relevant to your current needs. Mark it somehow. Ideally, this will be your big avoidance. However, sometimes time-sensitive items need to be tackled first.

Each item you establish as a priority is like a compass reading, enabling you to progress ever closer toward your final destination. Even if you choose to ignore certain items, at least you now know what they are. Only you can decide your path. There's one more small but essential thing to do before you start working on a task.

STEP 4: SCHEDULE A TIMEBOX (TO MAKE PROGRESS ON YOUR NORTH STAR GOAL).

Find a 30-minute slot in your calendar, preferably today, but certainly as soon as humanly possible, and create a block for thinking about or working on the next step toward your most important strategic goal. This approach works wonders for items that have long-term value but are not terrifically urgent. The point here is to feed your future. Research consistently shows that humans underestimate what they can accomplish if they chip away at something a little bit at a time, and, on the flip side, overestimate what they can accomplish when they're pressed for time.

So, "commit to yourself to dedicate time towards the goal, don't kid yourself about completing the goal. The promise is in allocation of time towards forward progress and a commitment to apply yourself."[8] All of the remaining items will become part of a continuously updated list of longer-term

7. Stephen R. Covey, A. Roger Merrill, and Rebecca R. Merrill, *First Things First* (New York, NY: Simon & Schuster, 1994).
8. Used with permission by Scott Sehlhorst.

items, your *backlog*. When the time is right, you'll repeat the previous process with those items.

STEP 5: WORK ON YOUR BIG AVOIDANCE.

Take a deep breath, exhale slowly, and then dig in. If you can afford to, start with your big avoidance, taking strict care not to multitask. Challenge yourself and see if you can complete, or chip away at, whatever you've identified as your top A1 priority—and nothing else. In my experience, completing your big avoidance, or at least making significant progress on it, is a surefire way to jumpstart your motivation. That said, if you do tackle your big avoidance, don't wait too long to take care of other items that need to be started or completed today.

The Power of the Boot

Why does this approach work so well? Perhaps it's because in a commercial environment, "If you have more than three priorities, then you don't have any."[9] The bottom line is this: Organizing your day around a small number of priorities improves your chances of investing your energy and time on the right things and getting back to work if and when you've been knocked off-task.

This doesn't mean that everything else you have on your plate is irrelevant. Even if you have a l-o-n-g backlog of other potential priorities, your ability to zero in on these three—just three!—items will set you free immediately.

Some people are naturals when it comes to setting goals and making checklists. However, if you're the kind of person who just prefers to let things happen and doesn't derive much joy from scratching off checklist items, then you will appreciate only needing to pinpoint three things every day. Like it or not, prioritizing depends on being explicit, which means writing things down.

Probably unsurprisingly, there are an infinite number of variations of the Morning Boot Routine. People customize it to make it their own. But some version of this time-tested, repeatable process can be the key to taking focused, purposeful action where the effects compound quickly over time.

---

9. Tony Hsieh, *Delivering Happiness: A Path to Profits, Passion, and Purpose*, read by Tony Hsieh (Hachette Audio, 2010), Audible audiobook, unabr., 8 hr., 17 min.

The main difference between a full-blown personal productivity practice like GTD and the Morning Boot Routine is that the latter gives you a mental scalpel that cuts to the heart of the most valuable aspect of GTD, which is to "organize our days around a small number of discrete objectives."[10]

I suggest you do the Morning Boot Routine...well, every morning. Preferably first thing on every weekday. By "first thing," I mean before you scan your emails and calendar, open your text messages, scroll through your social media stream, and especially—*especially*—before you fall into a black hole of news headlines. In my experience, the morning time is when your head is the clearest, and you've yet to be weighed down by the day's frenzy of activities.

Embracing the Morning Boot Routine before you engage with the outside world reduces the chance that you will activate your fight-or-flight response. This is crucial because cortisol, the hormone that triggers that emotional response, will also narrow your focus and cause you to lose sight of the bigger and often far more beautiful picture.

Even so, some people's heads are clearest in the evening right before they go to bed. If you can relate, don't let me stop you. Do it as the last thing you do every day to be all set for the morrow.

As it turns out, science agrees with my recommendation. Prioritizing can be depleting. According to David Rock, the author of *Your Brain at Work*, prioritizing is one of the brain's most energy-hungry processes, and "after even just a few mental activities, you may not have the resources left to prioritize."[11] Maybe this explains why we're often reluctant to take the time.

Turning the need for prioritization into a habitual DEGAP practice—a disciplined and repeatable approach—requires a not-insignificant commitment and a lot of willpower, as well as a system and workflow to capture, process, curate, and act on what matters most. Once you've mastered the basics, it may be time to take your game to the next level. Here's how it's done.

10. Cal Newport, "The Rise and Fall of Getting Things Done," *The New Yorker*, November 17, 2020, www.newyorker.com/tech/annals-of-technology/the-rise-and-fall-of-getting-things-done

11. David Rock, *Your Brain at Work: Strategies for Overcoming Distraction, Regaining Focus, and Working Smarter All Day Long,* read by Bob Walter (HarperAudio, 2011), Audible audiobook, unabr., 9 hr., 42 min.

The Advanced Morning Boot Routine

Progressing beyond the basics and developing a more comprehensive set of priorities demands a more rigorous process than the five steps spelled out previously. With that in mind, here's a list of additional steps you can take to make a better list of potential priorities.

Adding these advanced steps will allow you to get the absolute maximum out of your Morning Boot Routine, all in service of shortening the gap between your present and desired states.

Advanced Step 1: Review and add items to your list.

Advanced Step 2: Perform a role-based scan.

Advanced Step 3: Review your calendar and communications.

Advanced Step 4: Identify items to research, read, or think about.

Advanced Step 5: Highlight commitments, dependencies, levers, and questions.

Advanced Step 6: Identify your avoidances, time-sensitive items, and strategic next steps.

Advanced Step 7: Rank your avoidances, time-sensitive items, and strategic next steps.

Advanced Step 8: Schedule a timebox (to make progress on your North Star goal).

Advanced Step 9: Work on your big avoidance (ideally).

Once you've finished and can see how items stack up against one another, you will have successfully set the stage to move from thought to action. You will have clear choices of what to focus on and the confidence to make new commitments both to yourself and others.

ADVANCED STEP 1: REVIEW AND ADD TO YOUR LIST.

For this advanced step, continue the Morning Boot Routine by reviewing your existing list of priorities and any backlog you may have. Add any new items you've captured or that have come to mind since the last time you worked through the Morning Boot Routine. You'll be working off this new and improved list.

ADVANCED STEP 2: PERFORM A ROLE-BASED SCAN.

A role-based scan is a way to check and make sure that you haven't missed any items which may be critical. The idea is to conjure up other stakeholders, other important people, groups, and teams in your life. Does thinking of them jog your memory? Can you come up with any new items related to those who are important to you or who may be affected by your priorities?

In your personal life, the most obvious ones might be your partner/spouse, parents, in-laws, siblings, and so on. In a professional context, however, you're likely to have a number of additional stakeholders whom you ought to consider.

By examining your "role" in other's lives, you will be able to see more clearly any previously expressed or implied commitments you've made to others, all of which are essential to keep in mind during the DEGAP habit. This is especially important because keeping (or missing) important commitments in your personal life can have positive or adverse effects on your professional life and vice versa.

Checking in with these imaginary external stakeholders prompts you to consider what's on your plate from other points of view, which you might have missed.

ADVANCED STEP 3: REVIEW YOUR CALENDAR AND COMMUNICATIONS.

Your calendar is a physical manifestation of choices you are making about what really matters to you, so it's worth taking stock of. Look at the meetings, conference calls, events, etc. that you recently participated in. Do you need to follow up on anything or with anyone? For upcoming appointments, is there anything you need to do to prep?

Now check your Sent folder and other clickstreams (emails, text messages, Slack messages, etc.). Scan any messages you've recently sent. Make sure that you haven't skipped any commitments you made.

ADVANCED STEP 4: IDENTIFY ITEMS TO RESEARCH, READ, OR THINK ABOUT.

In addition to your avoidances, time-sensitive items, and next steps toward your longer-term strategic goals, you might find it helpful to add items that contribute toward your intellectual and skills development. This step is about prioritizing information and learning. Consider sources of information such as books or articles, podcasts, videos, training workshops, webinars, self-paced courses, etc. Prioritizing learning and development is particularly valuable for people who trade on their expertise: for example, engineers, doctors, scientists, researchers, and consultants of all types who need to stay abreast of the latest discoveries and upgrade their skills and capabilities.

ADVANCED STEP 5: HIGHLIGHT COMMITMENTS, DEPENDENCIES, LEVERS, AND QUESTIONS.

Be sure to highlight commitments you've made or deadlines that are looming, with the understanding that they may increase the urgency of acting sooner rather than later. If one of your potential priorities involves output that other people are depending on you for, you'll probably need to elevate its priority.

The same goes for potential priorities that could get more difficult, complicated, or expensive the longer they are unresolved. You'll most likely need to elevate the priority of these items as well. For instance, the longer you wait to buy a conference pass, the more expensive it's likely to get.

In addition to clarifying individual items to tackle, it's worth taking some time to group items that go together naturally. Part of this involves paying special attention to items that can provide leverage for addressing other, related items downstream (think parent/child relationships). For example, creating a how-to manual for contacting new clients will overlap with getting new hires in the sales department up to speed.

Given their compounding effect, there's a good chance that these kinds of items deserve higher priority.

ADVANCED STEP 6: IDENTIFY YOUR AVOIDANCES, TIME-SENSITIVE ITEMS, AND STRATEGIC NEXT STEPS.

Try to pinpoint what you're avoiding, willfully ignoring, or procrastinating on. Be honest with yourself. Put an "A" to the left of any item you are avoiding. I'll say it again—identifying and working on your avoidances is the single most important concept in this book. So, if you take away nothing else from reading this book, give this deceptively simple but powerful technique a chance. You'll be happy you did.

Next, identify items that are truly time sensitive. These are items that have a high cost of delay. If you don't address them promptly, they might cause you to lose control of a timeline or force you to pay for waiting.

Put a "T" to the left of those items. Finally, identify the items that will help you make progress toward longer-term (but no less important) strategic goals. Put a "G" to the left of them. Now review your list and reword any item that isn't self-explanatory and actionable.

ADVANCED STEP 7: RANK YOUR AVOIDANCES, TIME-SENSITIVE ITEMS, AND STRATEGIC NEXT STEPS.

If you see more than one item with an "A," rank the list from most-to-least important. Write "1" next to your Biggest Avoidance (e.g., the item with an A that's ranked as most important). Now, do the same thing for items with a "T" next to them. Then write "2" next to the item that's most urgent or pressing.

Repeat this process one more time, identifying the item whose completion is most essential for making progress on your strategic goals. Mark this item with a "3." After you've ranked your items, pressure-test your list. Again, be honest with yourself. Do these top three items truly reflect your highest priorities? If so, great. If not, reflect on what you've missed and refactor your list.

ADVANCED STEP 8: SCHEDULE A TIMEBOX (FOR PROGRESS ON YOUR NORTH STAR GOAL).

Finally, schedule a 30-minute slot in your calendar, preferably the same day to protect time you'll need to think about, plan, or make progress on the next action step toward your most important strategic goal. Again, the remaining items related to your North Start goal become part of your backlog.

ADVANCED STEP 9: WORK ON YOUR BIG AVOIDANCE (IDEALLY).

People often find that a well-prioritized list creates a shocking amount of clarity. Having such clarity, though, begs for action. But not just any kind of action—rather, effective action. To make the shift smoothly, you'll need to determine what you're going to tackle first.

If you can afford to defer your time-sensitive priority by a half-hour or so, the most effective first move is tackling your big avoidance. If at all possible, focus exclusively on it for roughly 30 minutes before you do anything else. And challenge yourself to complete it in the time you have. If that's not possible, make a concerted effort to chip away at it and make measurable progress.

Some people discover that shifting from thought to action is relatively easy once they've finished the Morning Boot Routine. This is particularly true after they've "bellied up to the bar" as they say and admitted at least to themselves what they've been avoiding.

But let's be real. Not everybody is so gung-ho. It's not uncommon for folks to stumble at this transition. Someone once told me that procrastination is not a personal productivity or time management problem, but rather an emotional regulation challenge. In other words, just knowing what's most important and admitting (to yourself) what you're avoiding isn't always enough to get over the emotional hurdle to get started. We're dealing with the human psyche here. And the struggle is real.

Faced with emotional friction, obstacles, and the overwhelming feeling of having "too much to do"—aka the demand to make difficult or painful trade-offs—the path of least resistance is sometimes to retreat into yourself rather than muster up the energy, courage, and fortitude to do battle with the demons of "maybe later."

But interestingly, it turns out that completing (or making significant progress) on a big avoidance offers a powerful reward on its own. It releases pent-up energy, a sense of aliveness, and bottled-up enthusiasm to dive into other projects, commitments, and work.

So, if you find yourself struggling to commit to working on your big avoidance, I suggest you consider giving it a try before you write it off. When I get stuck, a cheap trick I employ is to outline a plan for a plan, essentially a *very* short number of steps that I would need to do to start getting traction. In addition, there are a plethora of excellent resources on how to overcome procrastination. This can even include finding an accountability partner, a life or executive coach, or even talk therapy.

Push yourself a bit. Decide and commit to focusing on the top items on your list—*especially* on what you're avoiding. Chances are you'll find yourself saying, "Well, you know, that wasn't too hard," and then move on to the next thing.

Finally, as if this weren't enough, new items (potential priorities) of all types will inevitably pop up like a game of Whack-a-Mole. When (not if) this happens, remember you have three good options. The good options include:

- Take a moment to understand the new items and determine if and how they fit into your existing hierarchy of priorities.

- "Guesstimate" the relative priority of new items (assuming that you trust your skills in evaluating this) and adjust your existing priorities to accommodate new ones.

- Continue to focus on what you've already defined as a priority and add the new item(s) to a backlog of items to evaluate later.

You'll make the best choice by constantly asking yourself, "What's the value of doing X instead of doing Y?" (where X and Y are competing priorities). Or "What is the cost of *not* doing or delaying Z?" (where Z is the new item vying for your time and attention).

The worst option is to react to the new items without first considering the costs. This is how people lose control of the timeline. Ultimately, it's up to you. You're the decider.

10

Team Priorities

Everybody is part of some kind of team. Whether it's coworkers, members of a committee, or even participants in an ad hoc group, everyone collaborates with other people to establish a shared set of priorities and execute them. This reality means that you must be more intentional and explicit about the process of prioritizing. It's even more true when the stakes are higher, the team is larger, and the potential list of priorities (and consequences) is longer.

In this chapter we'll look at prioritizing from a team/group perspective. Note, though, that the focus here is on the relatively narrow process of prioritizing as a team and not on the ins-and-outs of collaborating effectively while on one. This means that the chapter sidesteps topics such as how to facilitate a meeting, resolve conflicts, harmonize wildly different opinions, etc. Instead, you'll learn what successful, episodic prioritization looks like within a team setting.

In contrast to prioritizing solely for yourself, prioritizing in a team setting often necessitates that you get more granular and dive deeper into the nitty gritty details of *how* you set priorities. It also typically requires using more quantifiable approaches.

If you're like most workers, there is a seemingly infinite range of circumstances and scenarios in which your team will be forced to figure out what their priorities are. But where do you begin? There are hundreds of frameworks, sorting techniques, simulations, and other methods you could use.

This was the exact situation I faced in 2016, when I was VP of Product & Design at AllClear ID, the Austin-based identity protection products pioneer. We had recently wrapped up our work helping Anthem Blue Cross Blue Shield deal with a national news-making data breach that impacted over 80 million people.[1] The work was tough, and the hours were grueling. Fresh on the heels of this massive mop-up, I was appointed to lead the company's Culture Team. My mandate was to improve employee initiative and satisfaction—and, by extension, our customer Net Promotor Score.[2]

Even if the particulars of your predicament(s) are different, I'm willing to bet the overall contours are not. Maybe it's a special project your boss drops on your plate, or perhaps an unexpected opportunity that lands in your lap. Or maybe it's something that, on the surface, seems ridiculously simple, like choosing the winner for a scholarship or award. Whatever the circumstance, I'm a firm believer that the same principles and tools that helped me and the AllClear ID Culture Team prioritize projects and people in 2016 can help you, too.

In the next few sections, I'll walk through my experience at AllClear ID to demonstrate the effectiveness of setting and executing strong team priorities. Among other highlights, you'll learn about a versatile and powerful prioritization tool called Simple Weighted Scoring.

1. Dan Munro, "Anthem Selects AllClear ID for Identity Theft Protection Service," *Forbes*, February 16, 2015, www.forbes.com/sites/danmunro/2015/02/16/anthem-selects-allclear-id-for-identity-theft-protection-service/?sh=1e9f76b5b4f4
2. Fred Reichheld, *The Ultimate Question: Driving Good Profits and True Growth* (Boston, MA: Harvard Business School Press, 2006).

Celebrating Unsung Heroes

AllClear ID was generally known for its excellent customer service and large-scale managed services. Before its identity protection business was acquired by the Experian credit bureau in 2019, AllClear ID helped organizations like Anthem Blue Cross Blue Shield, Home Depot, Sony Corporation, and the Department of Homeland Security respond successfully to data breaches. By some measurements, its work touched a sizable portion of the U.S. population at various points in time.

I had boomeranged back to AllClear ID in 2016 after my nearly four-year tour of duty at Rackspace. Bo Holland, the founder/CEO of AllClear ID, had found himself in a tight pinch. His CTO had quit unceremoniously, walking out the door with the intellectual keys to the technology platform, leaving Bo with one hot mess of tangled spaghetti, as they say in the software industry. And all of this while the CEO was under crushing pressure to scale up due to the increasing frequency and size of malicious corporate data breaches.

I had joined the company, originally named *Debix*, roughly ten years earlier. Bo had inspired me to leave PDI/DreamWorks to help design AllClear ID's first product offering. His prescient vision was to give consumers more control over their financial lives by enabling them to lock and unlock third-party access to their credit bureau history files. This would be done via multifactor authentication in the form of one-time passcodes (OTP) on users' mobile phones. We worked long hours on the hardwood chairs overlooking the water at Mozart's Coffee in Austin making this vision a reality.

Having returned to the company a decade later, my mission was now to help the organization become a high-reliability organization (HRO). The concept is especially popular among healthcare organizations (hospitals, administrators, and ancillary service providers). American Data Network, a company that helps healthcare-related organizations incorporate best practices into managing care, defines high-reliability organizations as "organizations that operate in complex, high-hazard environments for extended periods without serious accidents or catastrophic failures.... While high reliability is often thought of as effective standardization of processes, an HRO is better defined as a condition of persistent mindfulness within an organization."[3]

This being the case, one of my primary goals was to fortify our technology, processes, and culture so we could avoid the kinds of catastrophic failures our clients experienced. We were terrified that if we fell victim to a data breach ourselves, potential future clients would lose faith in our ability to keep them safe. So, I began by modernizing our core technology platform and upgrading our business processes, along the way observing first-hand just how critical our people were to keeping our systems running, performant, and secure.

After yet another day of observation, I had one of those inspiration light-bulb moments: we should create a special award to celebrate the employees who were doing the yeoman's work of making other employees' lives easier and better all around. I proposed that the company honor and reward these difference-makers, those people who were sniffing out and crushing problems before they happened, at our annual all-hands meeting. I also wanted to celebrate the unsung heroes in the most high-profile way possible. I imagined a cool trophy and a fat cash bonus to be awarded to one employee for toiling tirelessly behind the scenes.

The trophy and bonus were a nice way to say thanks, sure, but the deeper purpose was to create a powerful incentive for those who were putting themselves on the hook by taking initiative and addressing festering problems or mitigating risks that hadn't been identified or properly prioritized. At any given moment, our systems were supporting over a hundred million Americans, and the frequency and size of data breaches were unrelenting, as you can probably imagine. Keeping our systems up and running 24x7x365 was imperative; as the saying goes, failure simply wasn't an option. I also wanted to reward people who were proactive and who prevented disasters, rather than ones who responded to and fixed disasters. I specifically wanted to avoid doing what most organizations do when they want to recognize employee effort, which is to reward people for "jumping through fiery Cheerios," as Brian Fitzgerald, the former SVP of Worldwide Operations for Intuit, likes to call after-the-fact heroics.

---

3. "The Ultimate Guide to Becoming a High Reliability Organization + Free Tools to Help Build Your HRO and Measure Progress," American Data Network, July 8, 2021, https://blog.americandatanetwork.com/the-ultimate-guide-to-becoming-a-high-reliability-organization-plus-free-tools-to-help

To create an award that mattered, I'd have to build a team. One that would showcase upstream thinking, creative problem-solving, and, in particular, what humble (and successful) collaboration would look like. And then we'd have to decide what mattered.

Senior leadership loved the idea. The challenge was figuring out how to transform it from a rough concept into reality—and then select a first-time winner. In other words, I had to figure out our priorities.

The Team's Challenge

From the get-go, AllClear ID's Culture Team recognized the need for a thoughtful approach to this effort. Because the intent behind the award was to inspire employees throughout the year, they would have to have confidence that the process of selecting a winner was fair. This meant the methodology for identifying and selecting candidates and ultimately choosing a winner had to be transparent and easy to understand for all involved.

There was some added complexity as well: the process itself had to be repeatable. That meant our charge wasn't just coming up with "the answer," but coming up with a process that would come up with an answer in the future that would be different, one after that, and so on.

All of this sounded good in theory. But as I stared and stared at a blank whiteboard, it wasn't exactly obvious where to start. The award was brand-spanking new. There was no playbook to follow. Getting to "done done" was going to take a lot more than just picking a winner.

It required creating a prioritization playbook from scratch that addressed five critical objectives. Our process had to do the following:

- Make complete sense to everybody in the company, from frontline support reps to the senior leadership team.
- Accommodate multiple, yet-to-be-defined evaluation criteria and differing opinions as to the value of a candidate's contribution.
- Handle a potentially large number of prospective candidates.
- Produce results that were immune from personal bias and managerial politics.
- Be repeatable for a future Culture Team when it was time to pick a new Unsung Hero.

In a nutshell, we needed more than a magical Hogwarts Sorting Hat. We needed a way to close the gap between the *idea* of an award and an actual award, which meant having just enough structure and a workflow to ensure that we didn't miss or inadvertently skip critical steps that might bite back later on. Simple Weighted Scoring offered us just that.

Introducing Simple Weighted Scoring

Simple Weighted Scoring lets you use basic math to calculate first-order priorities. It works well—especially for teams— because it's, well, *simple* enough to account for common circumstances yet sophisticated enough to cope with fairly complex ones, too.

It can be a good alternative when visual frameworks or other sorting techniques, such as those covered earlier, don't fit the bill for various reasons. It's well-suited for straightforward planning or decision-making contexts, where the use of oversubscribed scoring methods such as RICE (reach x impact x confidence/effort) are unlikely to lead to great outcomes. It's also a good option when more sophisticated or truly quantitative techniques aren't required or particularly helpful.

For instance, imagine that you're on the hunt for a human transcription service that can turn an interview into text. In your process of evaluating options, you'll need to consider three criteria: speed, cost, and accuracy. If you want it fast and cheap, accuracy will suffer. If you want it accurate and fast, though, it will be expensive. And if you want it cheap and accurate, it will take longer.

There are always trade-offs to be made. The trick is deciding what the relative balance of these factors needs to be and how that balance will affect the results you want. Simple Weighted Scoring offers an easy way to balance these trade-offs. Plus, it's very systematic, predictable and, like any well-designed science experiment, repeatable. This makes it a perfect choice for teams.

Here's a basic example of what a Simple Weighted Scoring scorecard might look like:

TABLE 10.1 SIMPLE WEIGHTED SCORING SCORECARD
EXAMPLE

WEIGHT	CRITERION #1 35%	CRITERION #2 25%	CRITERION #3 40%	TOTAL
Item A	5	1	5	4
Item B	2	4	1	2.1
Item C	1	5	1	2
Item D	4	1	2	2.45

Here's the fairly simple math behind the scorecard:

- Each criterion gets a weight expressed as a percentage (with the total sum of the criteria equaling 100%).

- Each potential item to be prioritized is scored using a simple scale (e.g., 1–5).

- The calculated total score for each item determines its rank relative to other items.

Prioritizing this way is *quasi-* rather than *truly* quantitative.[4] This is because the values (weights) you assign to criteria are, in truth, subjective, even though they show up numerically (as a percentage). Still, using percentages to reflect different weights for different criteria helps teams make progress because it removes a bit of the mystery from the process of prioritizing.

Simple Weighted Scoring might look more complicated to some people than it actually is in practice. And scorecards *can* get complicated, but they don't have to be big, complex machines to work brilliantly. You don't need to be a spreadsheet wizard either, as the previous example demonstrates. However, you will find it easier to build a scorecard if you're comfortable with basic spreadsheet formulas.

---

4. Despite what you may have heard, there is an important place for the quasi-quantitative. Paul Henderson, VP of Business Operations at Proofpoint, told me that for most decision points, expecting truly quantitative data—and waiting until it arrives before making a decision—can be a fool's errand, "In practice, only a few management teams are willing to invest the time, effort, and money in developing truly usable quantitative models. When they do, they are still subject to GIGO (garbage in, garbage out) if the individual decision elements have not been vetted and normalized. To make decisions, it's better to do something right now, validate assumptions, and update plans as new information arrives than it is to generate a model with three decimal places of precision but questionable accuracy."

A major benefit of using Simple Weighted Scoring is that it lets you show your work. Each step is in your face. Thus, differences in opinion about criteria (which represent *what's* important) or weight (which signals *how* important each criterion is) can't lurk in the shadows, implied or unaccounted for. Since the process is out in the open, not only do team members have ample opportunity to negotiate for what they believe is important, they have a responsibility to do so.

Let me be up front and say that some people take issue with numerical methods such as Simple Weighted Scoring. In their view, hard numbers can give the appearance of being precise and exacting. But numbers alone don't tell the whole story. Paul Iverson, SVP of System Architecture for productOps, Inc., said that another place that people get into traps is that "numerical or quantitative methods let people hide decision-making behind how the numbers stack up. If they can put numbers on it, they think they can absolve themselves of decision-making responsibility. They just pick the thing with the higher number. And these approaches can also lend themselves to 'gaming the system' to get the answer they wanted."

This attitude is especially prevalent in product design and development environments where "numerical prioritization methods are controversial, and some experienced product people feel this left-brain approach can be misleading, arguing that it [provides] a false sense of confidence in math," in the words of the authors of the book *Product Roadmaps Relaunched*.[5]

I think this is a reasonable critique. That said, I also agree with Paul Henderson that the perfect (truly comprehensive, resource-intensive assessment models) is often the enemy of the good-enough (tools like Simple Weighted Scoring), especially when it comes to setting priorities.

At any rate, while the downsides of Simple Weighted Scoring are certainly worth keeping in mind, these issues weren't present with the AllClear ID's Culture Team. For us, Simple Weighted Scoring seemed like the right tool for the job. But even after we agreed on which prioritization tool we would use, we still had to make the transition from theory to practice.

---

5.   C. Todd Lombardo et al., *Product Roadmaps Relaunched* (Sebastopol, CA: O'Reilly Media, 2017).

Creating the Unsung Hero Playbook

The Culture Team experimented with Simple Weighted Scoring until a portrait of the award and what it would take to earn it began to emerge. It helped us figure out what our task entailed and potential criteria to focus on. It gave the Culture Team a strong starting point.

But despite its utility, we eventually realized it didn't quite provide an end-to-end solution for the unique challenge we were facing, which also—crucially—involved creating a playbook to share with future teams. For example, it didn't define the deeper purpose behind the Unsung Hero award. Nor did it spell out the details of what "success" actually looked like.

For Simple Weighted Scoring to answer these questions, it needed to be bulked up to establish the following: a set of criteria, percentage weights (for those criteria), and a scoring model.

That's when I suggested developing an Unsung Hero Playbook, a five-step process for determining all of the above. This playbook helped the team figure out what success looked like in concrete terms and what criteria, among many dozens of possibilities, *really* mattered—in other words, what values we should prioritize when it came to "performance."

As you read about these steps, I encourage you to apply them to a situation that's personally relevant to you, even if just informally or in your head.

STEP 1: DEFINE SUCCESS.

Before you start just about any new task or project, it's essential to figure out what success ought to look like. You can think of this step as part of engaging in the DEGAP process. "Measure twice, cut once," as my grandfather, a furniture maker, liked to say.

In a group setting, getting a hazy picture out of your collective heads and sharpening it with words is a surefire way to get the process rolling. It also allows you to easily adjust the picture as necessary until you and your teammates can agree that it's sound.

The Desired Outcome model, introduced in Chapter 5, is a perfect tool for accomplishing this. It's excellent for making sure that you are crystal-clear about what you're doing, why you're doing it, and whether your results will provide sufficient evidence of success.

In this context, the Desired Outcome model is a tactical tool you can use for any project to improve your chances of hitting the center of the target. It vastly improves the odds that your efforts will be directionally correct, regardless of what you're trying to accomplish. The last thing you want to do is start off in the wrong direction, do a lot of work, and then arrive at the wrong place.

In practice, most of the leverage you get from the Desired Outcome model comes from the fact that it forces you to answer three essential questions. Taken together, these will not only reveal what people think is required or expected but will also spell out the deep reason for or benefits of each. Once you have succinct answers, you can shift gears and start doing the "real" work of progressing further into the DEGAP process.

With this in mind, here's how the AllClear ID Culture Team applied the Desired Outcome model in Table 10.2.

TABLE 10.2 DESIRED OUTCOME MODEL TOP-3 QUESTIONS

	DESIRED OUTCOME QUESTION	ANSWER
1	What is wanted or needed?	A winner for the Unsung Hero Award.
2	What are the benefits of having it?	Confidence in our ability to present an inspiring award at the upcoming all-hands meeting and a goal that provides an incentive to employees to be proactive and solve problems before they occur.
3	How will we know when we have completed the project? [Evidence of success]	When we have one employee name, a list of runners-up, and a selection process we can explain without performing an interpretive dance. This information must be discovered in time to order (and receive) a trophy, get budget approval (and a cash prize from the CEO), and get on the agenda for the upcoming all-hands meeting.

The bottom line? The team needed to pick a winner in time to prepare for the upcoming all-hands meeting. This meant selecting an Unsung Hero who represented the spirit of the award unambiguously. Additionally, the Culture

Team felt it was essential that when the CEO announced the winner, none of the other employees would gasp in horror, suspicious that the process of selecting a winner was rigged. Given the importance of this priority, the team turned its attention to the development of the scorecard that each candidate would be evaluated against.

Accordingly, the next step was to determine how employees would compare potential award candidates against each other. It was time to identify selection criteria.

STEP 2: CREATE CRITERIA (OR GOOD CRITERIA/BAD CRITERIA).

Once we had our definition of success via the Desired Outcome model, the next step involved figuring out how items (in this case, the award candidates) should be evaluated. As you may well know from your own experience, when people decide they want to do something, early on they're often not very precise about what success looks like.

What happens in these kinds of circumstances is that people start brainstorming about potential priorities with vague intentions, fuzzy concepts, or rough thematic ideas. And, as they think more deeply about what's most important and, as they get closer to the problem they are trying to solve, criteria start bubbling up to the surface.

For this reason, it's important not to be dismissive of rough ideas early on, which are often very general. You'll get something you can sink your teeth into eventually as you continue to think things through.

Here's an example. During quarterly business planning, the AllClear ID senior leadership team focused on "bigger," "safer," and "faster" as general organizing themes. Bigger represented initiatives, projects, and other investments that gave the company a way to manage larger clients successfully. But "bigger" itself wasn't measurable—it was just a concept or *theme*. As a result, the leadership team couldn't use "bigger," "safer," or "faster" as criteria. Each theme had to be translated into a more concrete, measurable criterion. For instance, one of these quantifiable criteria ended up being "increases flexible capacity," which was specific enough and measurable in the context of AllClear ID's identity protection business to reflect "bigger."

Translating general themes into the specific criteria is a common task you have to perform in the prioritization process. It's how you make sure that you can measure what you have. It enables people with different perspectives and opinions to assign percentages or harder numbers to various priorities.

This is exactly what happened with the Unsung Hero Award. Think back to the intent behind the award. The original idea had embedded the general concepts we needed to start with: *toiling tirelessly behind the scenes*, *taking initiative* and *mitigating previously unseen risks*, *showcasing upstream thinking*, *creative problem-solving*, and *humble collaboration*. These were just general concepts. To pinpoint a set of criteria that the Culture Team could use in a Simple Weighted Scoring scorecard, they needed to translate the intent of the award (the themes) into specific values by which they could judge how well each candidate measured up (the criteria).

And this is what they did. "Mitigating previously unseen risks" translated into Scope of Impact, to which they assigned a score of one to five (one being the lowest). "Taking initiative" translated into Sought Forgiveness (notably, rather than approval). And upstream thinking translated into Foresight, which could be estimated using time data. Once the team defined the specific evaluation criteria, they could move on to the process of assigning weights to each criterion.

STEP 3: ASSIGN WEIGHTS TO CRITERIA.

For the Prioritization Matrix to work properly, each criterion needs its own measure of importance or weight. To do this, it's often helpful to start by Stack Ranking the themes to gain consensus on the relative importance of each criterion. Which one is most important? Which one matters the least?

The members of the Culture Team quickly agreed that demonstrating foresight and initiative to prevent a serious problem from occurring was extremely important. In fact, this quality was far more valuable than the ability to "solve" a problem that had already occurred. Once that was established, they moved on to the next ranking.

Each weight was expressed as a percentage relative to its level of importance. When you do this, any range of numbers is fine: 1–100, 100–1000, etc.—as long as you use the same range for all items and they map to percentages that total a hundred percent. Next, you'll assign a relative weight to each criterion.

Here's what the matrix looked like for us.

TABLE 10.3 STACK-RANKED AND WEIGHTED CRITERIA

WEIGHT	THEME/INTENT (REORDERED BY IMPORTANCE)	STACK-RANKED CRITERIA
30%	Upstream thinking	Foresight
25%	Taking initiative	Sought "forgiveness" instead of approval
20%	Creative problem-solving	Applied appropriate intervention strategy
15%	Humble collaboration	Peer-based recognition
10%	Mitigating unseen risks	Scope of potential impact
=100%		

See how the scorecard is starting to come together? It may look simple, but if so, it's deceptive. A lot of thought, discussion, and debate went into this!

STEP 4: DEVELOP A SCORING MODEL.

After you've listed the criteria, linked them to some sort of quantifiable range, and established a percentage weighting factor, the scorecard itself will be done.

However, you won't be able to use it until you have a scoring model, which, ideally, team members will agree on without reservation.

The goal of this step is to establish a point system for assigning numbers that can be used to judge items (in our case, candidates) in apples-to-apples fashion. This process requires establishing a range of numbers within which a given item (an award candidate) will rate.

How the scoring model works is straightforward. But, if like me, you're not brilliant at math, go slowly here. Take a criterion such as foresight, which has a weight of 30% in the previous chart. Imagine the foresight score for a given candidate is 5. When the scorecard calculations run, you would see that 30% of 5 equals 1.5.

This, it turns out, is one of the raw numbers that will become part of that candidate's total score. But more on that later. For now, the question is: what does a 5 actually mean?

That's part of what the scoring model spells out. Is 5 high or low? Assuming the ranges go from 1 to 5, what does each level mean? Well, it depends on the criterion you're talking about. For us, foresight represented upstream thinking: How far in advance somebody foresaw a potential problem that the current of time was all but guaranteed to send downstream, at which point it would ultimately become an actual problem.

So, the foresight criterion was represented in calendar time: hours or days, weeks, months, quarters, to infinity and beyond. Somewhat arbitrarily, we decided that one equaled hours, two equaled days, three equaled weeks, and so on.

At this point, your team also needs to take the time to spell out the numeric scale (and meaning) for each criterion. Without doing this, you won't be able to compare items against each other and arrange them in order of importance.

Let's look at a sample scorecard. The final column is an example of the AllClear ID Culture Team's scale. You may recall that for a criterion to be valid, it must have an attribute and a value. Take the theme of upstream thinking for instance. We decided to label the criterion "foresight." We assigned the attribute of time. And we agreed on the values in the Scale column in Table 10.4.

When you work through this process, remember that getting team members on the same page about the scoring model is key. For example, the most common cause of failure is not gaining consensus on a model when it comes to Simple Weighted Scoring.

In this scenario, the model ends up being confusing at best or completely meaningless at worst. All of which is to say, it's essential to avoid moving forward before all team members have completely bought into the scoring model. Get firm agreement in advance or renegotiate the model if need be. Go slow to go fast.

TABLE 10.4 ALLCLEAR ID UNSUNG HERO SCORING MODEL

WEIGHT	THEME/ INTENT	STACK- RANKED CRITERIA	MEASURE	SCALE	
30%	Upstream Thinking	Foresight	How far into the future?	1	Hours
				2	Days
				3	Weeks
				4	Months
				5	Quarters+
25%	Taking Initiative	Sought "forgiveness" rather than approval	Level of "forgiveness" required	1	NA
				2	Minor
				3	Medium
				4	Serious
				5	Possibly career ending
20%	Creative Problem-Solving	Intervention strategy	Scope of impact vs. solvability	1	Heads up
				2	Problem
				3	Predicament
				4	Crisis
				5	Extinction
15%	Humble Collaboration	Amount of recognition	Number and level	1	Peer(s)
				2	Direct sup.
				3	Multiple peers
				4	Mgmt. team
				5	Senior leaders
10%	Mitigating Unseen Risks	Potential impact	Business pain	1	Operations
				2	Cust. Support
				3	One client
				5	Multiple clients
				8	Compliance

STEP 5: FILL IN THE SCORECARD AND CALCULATE RESULTS.

After the Culture Team had nailed down the scoring model and gained consensus, they were ready to prioritize the candidates. In other words, it was time to build and populate a spreadsheet using the model. Next, they calculated each candidate's weighted score by multiplying the raw scores by each criterion's weight and adding up the resulting values. Then they added up the newly calculated score item by item, which brought them to the total score.

The team reviewed the process and results with the full senior leadership team. Unfortunately, I do not have a copy of the final score sheet to show how the other candidates lost out to Stephen. But take it from me, there was no question: Stephen Zemlicka, an IT systems administrator, represented the truest spirit of AllClear ID's first annual Unsung Hero Award.

Stephen had identified, without management direction, a festering problem deep within the AllClear ID platform and taken the appropriate steps to mitigate it with no drama or expectation of recognition. Congratulations again, Stephen.

Not only did the Culture Team manage to present a meaningful award to Stephen (along with a nice bonus), but it successfully built an enduring, repeatable process for identifying future Unsung Hero Awards.

Simple Weighted Scoring isn't perfect for every situation. But if you've got a team or group, and especially if they haven't worked together before, it gives you a straightforward recipe that everybody can follow.

At a minimum, it's a great tool to start a conversation with, even if you ultimately end up choosing a different sorting technique, visual framework, simulation, or other method. Simply by discussing how it works, you'll get people primed to think about criteria and how to quantify them.

Most teams can muddle through prioritizing a set of projects, problems, opportunities, or other items just once. But turning a team's prioritization process into a rigorous practice requires a repeatable system, a defined workflow, and new techniques.

This is the focus of the next chapter. You'll learn how episodic prioritization can help you balance competing interests and stay on track in the medium and long term. The product design and development fields are a great example of this. In both areas, new items are added constantly, and the relative value of existing items is reevaluated and reprioritized frequently. However, you don't have to work in either to benefit from prioritizing regularly.

11

Sustaining
Team Success

U nless a team already has an ongoing practice of prioritizing regularly, the question inevitably arises: When and how often should you be doing it? As the previous chapter showed, episodic events have specific beginnings and definitive endings, often leading to "fire-and-forget"-type decisions. There's generally no need to revisit or catalog and manage the items you didn't pursue, the ones that ended up on the cutting room floor.

This chapter looks at team priorities that are more permanent—priorities that require groups to consistently exchange information, participate in decision-making, and perform priority-related tasks. This arrangement is especially common among teams that contribute to the design, development, delivery, operation, and support of products and services of all types. Constantly evolving circumstances push teams to continually set and refresh their priorities.

We'll begin with a poignant example from my first job with a Silicon Valley startup, Virtual Vineyards. As you'll learn, although my colleagues and I did a great job of setting our initial priorities in preparation for our site launch, we missed a pivotal opportunity to manage our ongoing priorities over the long haul, much to our detriment. This example shows how teams (especially smaller ones) often go about prioritization the wrong way. And it uncovers some deeper truths about what you can do if your team has ongoing prioritization challenges.

Clear Purpose and Shared Priorities

Who would you bet built the first user-friendly, secure internet shopping cart? Amazon? eBay? PayPal? Odds are, you wouldn't put your money on a little company called Virtual Vineyards—but that's what happened, and I was right in the middle of it all.

Online shopping, as you know it today, began on January 24, 1995, in a cramped basement cellar in Los Altos, California. Virtual Vineyards (now Wine.com) went "live" at 8:57 in the morning when the webmaster (yours truly) removed the "Beta" GIF image from the homepage on the first secure retail store on the Web. It was, get this, roughly seven months before Amazon.com opened for business.[1]

Yours truly in the basement cellar "office" of Virtual Vineyards.

1. Russell Mitchell, "Safe Passage in Cyberspace," Bloomberg, March 19, 1995, www.bloomberg.com/news/articles/1995-03-19/safe-passage-in-cyberspace

On a crisp October day a few months earlier, the three founders, CEO Robert Olson, Master Sommelier Peter Granoff, and I—a guy who knew more about motorcycles and motor oil than wine—stood around the Olsons' kitchen island eating hors d'oeuvres and triple-cream brie. A bottle of Storybook Mountain Zinfandel lubricated the conversation. We aligned on three key priorities for the website launch. It would do the following:

- Educate visitors and help them learn about our products through compelling origin stories.

- Make online shopping easier than "dog-ear" ordering from a mail-order catalog.

- Give seamless customer experience precedence over technology constraints and limitations.

But that wasn't all. A secret that even the most diehard dotcom historians don't know about Virtual Vineyards is that it wasn't only about selling wine.

VV was, in effect, a subsidiary of our "real" startup, NetContents. The wine store was supposed to be part of an experiment to prove that people would buy specialty goods on the internet—more specifically, products that were differentiated primarily through the information about them (the intriguing background of the company, the people who produced it, and the origin story behind the product)—rather than package design and surface features and benefits. We called these kinds of goods, which didn't get much shelf space in larger stores, "information-rich products."

All sounds good, right? Well, this goal was never explicitly agreed to and, as a result, we neglected to spell out a top-level priority to manage it. We just assumed that if VV succeeded, we could use it as a model for selling anything online.

You probably know what happens when you make assumptions. Now think about what can happen when an entire unspoken business model rests on one.

This was the first time the three of us had all worked together. Robert and I had previously worked together in the Programming Products and CASE Tools group at Silicon Graphics, the pioneering Silicon Valley manufacturer of high-performance workstations, supercomputers, and software for professionals specializing in 3D graphics. Robert and Peter were related. They were family, which is often enough when it comes to doing business.

When a team is small and co-located and the list of objectives is short, the process of setting priorities is usually a snap. In our case, the purpose of the business was clear. We had a shared sense of what we were trying to accomplish and why. The idea was to make the experience of shopping on a computer as easy (or even easier) than perusing a mail-order catalog. So, talking through our goals, figuring out what mattered, and coming up with a short list of initial priorities wasn't tough.

We didn't give things a second thought. With half a million dollars in the bank from an eccentric investor, we were off to the races. We never considered the possibility that our priorities might change or get out of focus, so we didn't see the need to be more methodical or to commit to revisiting them later. After all, this is how most people do it.

We assumed everything was fine and went on with our jobs, noses to the grindstone. By late 1996, our little Silicon Valley startup was dubbed "one of the three internet darlings," along with CDNow and Amazon.com, by the *Economist*.[2] At the time, we thought Virtual Vineyards was a brilliant success. The model was working! But truth be told, we were failing.

We were so focused day-in and day-out on running and growing Virtual Vineyards that we didn't prioritize the process of prioritization. It's not like we didn't have a decent excuse (or so we thought). There were the super long hours; the relentless onslaught of new orders; operations and logistics; legal hurdles; customer questions; technology scaling; and new feature development. Attending to all of this made it tough—seemingly impossible—for us, as cofounders, to stay deeply aligned.

My conversations with Rob Reesor, Virtual Vineyards' lead engineer, continued to focus on pushing the technology infrastructure toward our initial vision of democratizing ecommerce. We would do this by enabling all sorts of merchants to build their own online stores. But as the wine business grew larger and took root, the yeoman's work that Peter, our esteemed Master Sommelier, was doing continuously fed new products and fresh content into an increasingly specialized model for selling wine online, an implementation that was slipping further and further away from Robert's initial vision.

2. "Suited, Surfing and Shopping," *The Economist*, January 25–31, 1997, p. 59.

It's not that any of us misunderstood the vision or original strategic priorities. But our day-to-day decisions were in response to the needs of the wine business rather than our North Star.

Robert, Peter, and I continually adjusted our priorities to accommodate what was happening in our little corner of the internet. The problem was that what was obvious to each of us was just a little bit different.

Meanwhile, Robert and the board of directors were sword fighting, figuratively speaking, about investment, resource allocation, and (as I was about to find out) the overall direction of the company.

Day-by-day, week-by-week, board meeting—board meeting, our respective long-term priorities—which, again, were never formally articulated, but lived inside each of our individual minds—slowly diverged.

Robert, the board of directors, and Peter leaned into the wine and specialty foods business. And the ecommerce platform team and I continued pursuing the original vision of enabling specialty retailing (to sell all kinds of products). And through it all, we never stopped hustling long enough to notice that our shared sense of purpose was approaching the point of no return, that we needed to talk to each other about how our priorities were drifting apart.

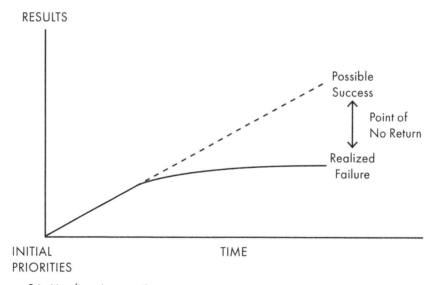

Priorities diverging over time.

On a warm June afternoon, I walked into Robert's Palo Alto office and closed the door. This would be the conversation that made it clear to us that our hive mind was gone—that there was no more group flow.

For reasons that weren't clear to me at the time, Robert informed me that he had made an executive decision to expand the scope of "wine store" to include specialty foods rather than continue building out a separate specialty food store.

"This will never work," I thought to myself. The approach was out of alignment with our current implementation strategy. It felt wrong, given my understanding of our original vision to enable specialty retailing online.

The fact is, I was blithely unaware of the challenges that Robert, as CEO, was having getting more investors on board and how legal challenges were costing too much time and money. Similarly, Peter, as Master Sommelier, and I never talked explicitly about how the wine and specialty food business had begun to take on a life of its own and now made more sense as a single store with a seamless unified catalog.

So, after a stinging conversation about how decisions were (and should be) made, I was done. Later that summer, after overseeing the integration of the wine and specialty products under the new moniker, Wine.com, I left my first startup.

In retrospect, my experience at VV shines a bright light on the power of priorities. But it sheds an even harsher light on the risks that can come from not being intentional and explicit when it comes to setting team priorities. Because we didn't stay tuned into what our priorities were and we didn't revisit them as they shifted and changed, the team eventually became unmoored. Each of us headed in slightly different directions. Wine.com survived. But it lost its mojo, and, crucially, its ability to continue innovating at a speed that would have allowed it to stay ahead of other nascent ecommerce companies who were nipping at our heels.

This is often how it happens. One day you're just standing around talking things out; the next thing you know, you're done. Some of the time it works out. Sometimes it doesn't. But here's the thing: when it doesn't turn out the way you hoped for, it's rarely obvious that the source of the problem was with the process of prioritization…or lack thereof. Standing around the table got us off to a great start. But as situations evolved and became more complex, wine and cheese were no longer good enough tools to realize business success.

Almost any team can prioritize a set of problems, risks, projects, opportunities, or tasks once. But developing, refining, and then relying on a *system* to prioritize and reprioritize continually requires a deeper commitment and a willingness for team members to hold each other accountable.

This is especially true for teams that work in constantly changing environments or are a part of a larger organization. In these contexts, new priorities pop up like a game of Whack-a-Mole, and team members must respond swiftly and resourcefully to the constant influx of new information and demands—or make the judicious decision to ignore them. Whatever the case may be. All of which is to say, teams that need to manage ongoing priorities will have to execute four key tasks:

- Develop a rhythm or cadence for prioritizing.
- Prioritize new tasks and reprioritize existing ones as needed.
- Create and manage backlog(s).
- Decide which items to select from the backlog.

Here's what you need to know about doing just this.

Priorities Have a Shelf Life

Knowing what I know now, I believe my cofounders and I probably should have revisited our top-level priorities at least once a month. This was the cadence of our board meetings, which was where strategic decisions were ratified. Although discussing them this frequently wouldn't have guaranteed success, chances are it would have improved the odds of our achieving our original long-term vision. At the very least, it would have helped us stay on the same page.

In a given environment, as the rate of situational change and tempo of a team (velocity of work) increase, so does the need to revisit priorities. This doesn't mean that the priorities necessarily have to change. But it does mean that teams ought to consider new inputs and information and determine whether it makes sense to reprioritize in light of them. And they ought to do this somewhat regularly, ideally at a set schedule.

There's a huge range of prioritizing and reprioritizing cadences. In life-or-death situations, teams may need to triage and reprioritize from moment to moment. And in highly operational environments, the setting and resetting of priorities typically happen once a day.

In environments where products and services are under development, prioritization typically takes place less frequently. Software development teams that favor being more agile do sprint planning every two or three weeks. Hardware development teams and teams working on complex physical systems like commercial construction revisit their formal priorities less frequently, in part because building tangible things just takes longer.

The point is that in any kind of environment where the stakes are high, day-to-day problems that have cascading consequences may prompt a flurry of rapid reprioritization but without much of a formal process. For instance, take the IT/Security Team at a data-breach response company like AllClear ID, which relied on daily huddles to determine what each team member's top priority was for that day, and whether they had successfully tackled it. Contrast this with somebody like Notre Dame professor and acclaimed lunar scientist Clive Neal, who is currently planning a NASA mission. His team may only need to revisit their mission "investigation" priorities once a year.

As a general rule, the more frequent the meetings, given a culture that genuinely encourages varied perspectives, the less likely that priorities will drift and goals will defocus. Frequent meetings promote greater transparency. Team members can see what's changing and what's not, as well as how things are flowing and connecting, thus allowing for near-immediate reprioritization, assumption-checking, and error correction if necessary. (Obviously, frequent meetings come with their own well-documented downsides. But by "meeting," I don't mean an hour-long assembly in an auditorium, just a meaningful, BS-free check in.)

Larger teams, especially those that are distributed geographically, may want to combine weekly check-ins and longer-term checkpoints every four to eight weeks. An excellent rule of thumb is this: if it's time to plan (or replan), then it's time to prioritize (or reprioritize). Not to put too fine a point on it, but priorities are a fundamental input of planning.

Think about the situation that you and your team are currently in. How static or dynamic is your environment? What about the velocity of work your team is doing—do your teammates agree on what's important and what's not? How frequently does it make sense to revisit your priorities? Too frequently, and nothing will seem to be changing. Too infrequently, and everything will be in flux.

Does Your Team Need an Upgrade?

If your team has already established a healthy practice for prioritizing and reprioritizing periodically, great—feel free to skip this section. If not, however, your team would do well to surface what's holding it back and preventing it from developing a repeatable practice of prioritization. To be sure, it's not always obvious or easy to talk about the kinds of things that may be preventing your team from going fast, doing better work, or winning. Being candid with anybody, especially your fellow team or group members, is always risky. You might offend them, or worse, they might say something unsettling. Plus, your feelings might get hurt.

Fortunately, there's an effective and relatively fun tool you can use to identify problems, avoid unnecessary confrontation, and deal with responses constructively. It's called *Speedboat*.[3] Although Speedboat is not exclusively for teams, it's a fun and effective framework for engaging a team and figuring out what's holding them back.

Using Speedboat to Speed Up Progress

Speedboat is a deceptively simple visual framework that utilizes the metaphor of a boat attempting to power through the water. It helps teams identify four essential elements that tend to hold members back from performing at their collective best. It prompts individual team members to express openly what is weighing their "boat" down (anchors); what's lurking under the surface that might cause problems (rocks); what could help the team accelerate (propellers); and what could save the team if it runs aground (life preservers).

Speedboat is perfect for gathering insights about performance, especially from fellow team or group members. There's a yin/yang relationship between speed and priorities. It's a lot easier to go fast with confidence if you know

---

3. Luke Hohmann, *Innovation Games* (Boston, MA: Addison-Wesley Professional, 2007).

what's most important…and what's not. While it's useful in many work contexts, it's particularly valuable for figuring out what might be preventing a team from prioritizing the process of ongoing prioritization.

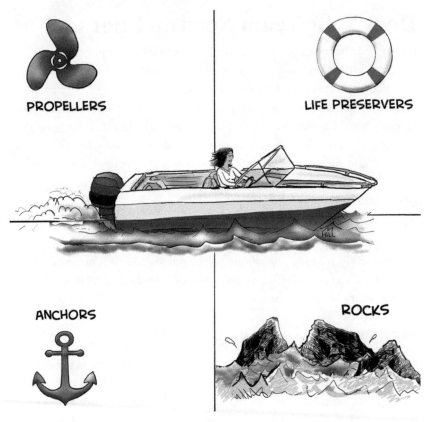

Identifying and prioritizing team impediments.

It works by giving individual members the space to reflect on what's genuinely most important and offering a more playful, low-stakes way to spell out the reasons their team isn't perfectly aligned. By prompting each member to externalize these factors and turn them into problems "out there," the process feels safer psychologically.

To that end, Speedboat often works best if individual team members first write down their own thoughts or feelings before sharing them openly. This is especially helpful for introverts and folks who bristle at having to deal with domineering personalities. And it is key for people who may have valuable insights but don't feel at ease blurting out their observations, concerns, or frustrations about the team's or an individual member's performance.

With more clarity about what's holding your team back from performing at its best, you'll be well positioned to decide which factors to focus on and make adjustments to as you pursue your vision of success. And once everyone on your team has a chance to offer their thoughts, you can collectively determine next steps to address obstacles to ongoing prioritization and work out a rhythm for doing so periodically.

Now, some people might think that using an innovation game like Speedboat is contrived. But had I known about Speedboat when I was at Virtual Vineyards, perhaps we would have found a way to stay more aligned. We lacked a framework for pinpointing our priorities, one that could have helped us articulate what was necessary to close the gap between our current implementation, the new strategic direction, and the future platform I envisioned—a system that would allow merchants to launch independently owned and operated online stores. Had we put our collective heads together and refreshed our priorities, I might be telling you a vastly different story. But we didn't.

So, ask yourself, what, if anything, is holding back your team from excelling? Does your team have a good way to prioritize collectively? Do you have a cadence that makes sense, given the environment you're operating in and the tempo of your team's work? What about your backlog(s)—are they prioritized so you can just pluck items and work on them? Do you need to develop any contingency plans or "life preservers?" Do you have one of those teams where everything is priority one? If so, you may have to think even more strategically when it comes to prioritizing effectively.

When Everything Is Priority One

The difficult truth is this: If everything is a priority, then nothing is. If your team had infinite time, attention, and resources, there'd be no need to shy away from trying to do everything. But it doesn't.

So, if everything is consistently treated as a top priority, it's a pretty strong indication that it's time for your team to reflect on and adjust how it operates. Doing so will help you avoid what Eric McGregor, a Sr. Product Manager, calls the "illusion of priorities," a situation:

"…where new Priority-Ones keep coming down the pike, but the older ones don't go away. So, you never really shift priorities. You just kind of now have a new one, too. The idea that you would stop doing something is the idea of losing.… If the team doesn't meet a goal, it's not because there are external factors or other really good reasons which may be very real; it feels more like you didn't meet your objective. And it seems like once an objective is stated but not completed, it is there forever."[4]

All of this probably sounds nice, at least in theory. But you may be wondering (with no small amount of irritation) how you're supposed to respond when your team is relentlessly overwhelmed and your manager, captain, or VP keeps dumping new problems or opportunities onto your already overflowing plate. What then?

Here's the challenge: When senior leaders bark an order or make an ask, a team is more likely to hear the request as a demand rather than a request (that is, something that might be negotiable). This is especially tough when your team is already swamped—three or four "top" priorities, each with its own timeline, dependency, and people. Your fantasy response is probably something along the lines of "NO!!!" But even in the best of circumstances, people don't like to give that response (or, for that matter, receive it). Saying no often intensifies people's worries about burning bridges or being perceived as someone who turns down supposedly exciting opportunities or novel experiences.

On the other hand, saying yes potentially comes with a huge set of liabilities. Saying yes to one request without saying no to another can, and often does, force a team into the unfortunate situation where constant firefighting becomes business as usual. The hazard of constant heroics is that it depletes the team's headroom, the flexible capacity required to handle additional unexpected problems. Prioritizing, unsurprisingly, falls by the wayside, along with any other task that doesn't immediately help put out the fire. Constant firefighting burns teams out. So, how can you or your team avoid finding yourselves in this untenable situation?

STEP 1: COMMIT TO COMMIT (OR NOT).

If your team is being pressed to take on too much, ask for the time you need—say, 24 hours—to clarify the request, huddle with your team, and

---

4. Used with permission by Eric McGregor.

figure out what's possible and what can be deferred. If humanly possible, do not agree either explicitly or implicitly to take on the new work. Instead, tell the requestor specifically when to expect a response from you about what your team can or cannot commit to. In other words, commit to committing to provide a considered answer. The key here is to respectfully acknowledge new requests without giving the impression that you've got them covered.

Creating this space gives you time to renegotiate competing commitments, uncover hidden assumptions or dependencies, and adjust relative priorities to accommodate the new request. As long as you're being straightforward, you may be surprised by the results of this new approach. William Ury, author of the *Power of a Positive No*, suggests that everybody, and especially leaders, "...prefers a clear answer, even if it's no, than continued indecision and waffling."[5] Only truly urgent circumstances or the most unreasonable bosses will forcefully demand that you leap before you look and take on more than you can handle. (Side note: If you find yourself consistently pressured to satisfy unreasonable bosses, it may be time to revisit Chapter 8, about applying the prioritization framework to a job search.)

Having created a small window of time to evaluate the request fairly, you and your teammates can figure out what success looks like and whether any existing priorities need to be adjusted or commitments renegotiated. I speak from experience when I say that even just a little time can go a long way.

STEP 2: PRIORITIZE OR REPRIORITIZE.

For a team to have a healthy, ongoing flow of high-quality work, it needs to establish a process for prioritizing and reprioritizing, a way to select items, and a robust backlog of (weighted) items to draw from. That's where the next sections come in. Properly managing and executing a backlog can be the difference between consistent team success or failure. Only once you understand what needs to be done will you know what could be done, for your boss or anyone else.

STEP 3: CLOSE THE LOOP.

Before you respond to the person requesting yet another priority one, make sure that your teammates are on the same page about what the requestor

---

5. William Ury, *The Power of a Positive No: Save the Deal Save the Relationship—and Still Say No*, NO-VALUE edition (New York, NY: Bantam, 2007).

actually wants. Tread carefully here, since what the person explicitly says they want may be very different from what they're expecting. Surface any important assumptions and identify questions that need to be addressed or answered and give them the space to offer their perspectives and opinions. Once your team understands what is wanted, why it is important, and how your stakeholders will judge success, you are in position to firm up the commitment—or reject it.

Creating and Managing Backlogs

But back to those backlogs, which are an essential element of regular (that is, no episodic) prioritizing, especially when teams are involved. The simplest definition of a backlog is a list of items to be evaluated for future consideration. Any items that don't make the final cut onto your list of active priorities should, in theory, tumble into your backlog. The fact is, if you don't put those items somewhere, you're probably going to forget some of them. Possibly many of them.

In product design and development environments, an idealistic backlog represents a single authoritative source for features, functions, and products that teams may work on in the medium to longer term. Realistically, however, such a backlog needs to be easy to filter and sort, based on various categories, criteria, or other attributes. If not, maintaining multiple, purpose-built backlogs will help your team stay sharply focused on what matters most. Either way, if your team has a backlog, maintain it vigilantly. Don't use it as a dumping ground for undefined work, unprioritized items, or random ideas that haven't been vetted. A backlog isn't a brainstorming session.

Depending on the types of items to be held on a backlog, the backlog itself may be a simple stack-ranked list, a Kanban or task board, a Scrum sprint backlog, or a spreadsheet that ranges from a Simple Weighted Scoring scorecard to something more sophisticated that lets you filter and pivot for different views based on themes, categories, tags, and multiple attributes.

(Incidentally, if your team is wondering whether or not you need a repeatable process to manage ongoing priorities, it's useful to note that the very existence of a backlog should make it clear that the answer is yes.)

ITEM A   TOP PRIORITY

ITEM B

ITEM C   PRIORITIES

ITEM D

ITEM E   BOTTOM PRIORITY

ITEM F

ITEM G

ITEM H   BACKLOG

ITEM I

Active priorities vs. backlog.

Backlogs were one thing we did right at Virtual Vineyards. Say what you will about the evolution of our business model—and I've said quite a bit—but our backlog systems were always top-notch. All of which gets at a larger truth about backlogs and their role in prioritization: having a highly functioning backlog system is necessary but not sufficient. As perfect as your system may be, it still needs to be guided in the right direction via the right inputs (i.e., priorities).

At Virtual Vineyards, we had three types of backlogs, which, in concert, allowed us to maintain an integrated set of priorities. They gave us a stream-lined queuing system to work from. It minimized the tendency to take on too much at once. And it helped maximize our focus on what mattered most. These backlogs included a working task list like a Kanban board that had a queue of projects and other items that were ready to go, a larger, holistic development backlog that contained items of all types, and our personal backlogs.

The working task list contained a list of force-ranked items in a queue, one primary item that required the team's undivided attention, and a growing list of completed items. This accomplished two important objectives: preventing our "one thing" from becoming "one more thing" and alerting anybody who was interested and could contribute to the most important work in progress.

	QUEUE	WORKING	DONE
1.	_____	_____	_____
2.	_____	_____	_____
3.	_____	_____	_____
4.	_____	_____	_____
5.	_____	_____	_____

The structure of our store's task list.

The larger, holistic development backlog contained a wide variety of items, including:

- Ideas for automating manual processes
- Potential new features and capabilities
- Software bugs and customer-experience defects
- Architecture improvements and technical debt
- Potential new products and content

Items in this list were ranked in terms of priority (high, medium, or low) and their estimated amount of work or effort and complexity (via T-shirt sizes: XS, S, M, L, XL, and 2XL).

Then we divided the development backlog into two, creating an active task list (in the form of a Kanban board) and a separate, general backlog to signal that the items in the task list queue were prioritized, appraised in terms of impact vs. effort, and ready to go. This meant there were no obvious dependencies that would prevent us from making progress once we started to tackle them.

Items that remained on the general backlog (not on the task list) weren't queued up. But they were prioritized, even if they still needed a certain amount of clarification, investigation, and so forth. Splitting the backlog into a task list and long-term backlog allowed us to make continual rapid progress because we could focus on the most important priority as a team and start working on the next most important items early. If any members of our design, engineering, or content teams got free early, they could select work from the task list or take time to work on personal priorities, which might include digging into the deeper backlogs.

Each of us had personal backlogs as well. Sometimes the items on our respective personal backlogs were in service of the team's longer-term opportunities and didn't directly affect anybody else, dependencies-wise. Most of the time, though, they intersected in one way or another.

Personal priorities feeding the task list.

The sketch just above illustrates how our personal priorities and task lists ended up rolling into a unified list of priorities and backlog. For instance, sometimes our customers asked for products that we did not stock. So, on my personal backlog, I maintained an array of "request groups" to track the demand for items that our customers wanted but we didn't have any immediate plans to source. When a request group hit critical mass—say, 25 requests for a wine without sulfites—I would share this information with Peter, whose responsibility included procuring new wines, specialty foods, and other related products.

If and when Peter agreed to take on a new request, I notified the customers on that list, and the request shifted from my personal backlog to Peter's so he could prioritize it among all of the other things he was juggling. Likewise, as items on Peter's personal backlog moved onto his list of active priorities, those items simultaneously moved onto our general store backlog so we could begin planning for them.

It was a manual process. But I figured out how to automate it. And a couple of years after leaving Virtual Vineyards, I founded a startup called Public Mind that provided a unified demand aggregation system "suggestion box" technology to capture, manage, and respond to unmet customer needs.

We managed our priorities this way to stay on task with what we truly needed to do, rather than getting sidetracked by pet projects or what we wanted or simply remembered to do. It helped us steer the boat and avoid getting distracted by our own special obstacles: the loudest voices telling us what to do, whether they were customers, suppliers, or even our own staff.

To pick priorities off the general backlog, we used a specialized version of Simple Weighted Scoring (introduced in the previous chapter) called *Weighted Smallest Job First* (WSJF). WSJF scores items higher if they are valuable but are smaller and will take less effort to complete. In this way, WSJF prioritizes work that will get done sooner because it moves faster through the development pipeline.

The main benefit of completing small, high-value items sooner is that they begin accruing value by being "in the market," so to speak, where they can be put to work for your customers and your business. Another benefit is that completing them often unblocks larger, even higher-value items. WSJF also happens to be an excellent way to understand the costs of delay.

By adding a Cost-of-Delay criterion to the Simple Weighted Scoring model, you can better understand the downside cost associated with waiting to act. So, it is a good model for evaluating opportunity cost when you have more items than capacity to execute. (Check out the Appendix for more information.)

Pruning Backlogs

To prevent your backlog from becoming a dumping ground or growing too unwieldy, your team will benefit from ongoing pruning. This term, which evokes deliberate and active maintenance to prevent things from getting out of control, is apt. In his book *Necessary Endings*, Henry Cloud explains that "The gardener intentionally and purposefully cuts off branches and buds that fall into any of three categories:

- Branches and healthy buds that are not the best
- Sick branches that are unlikely to heal
- Dead branches that are consuming space and light required for the healthy ones to thrive"[6]

The parallels with tasks and priorities are obvious. A useful backlog is prioritized and pruned. This means that individual items have been clarified, and that the team developing the priorities has evaluated the items to determine which ones are more or less important than the others. It also means that duplicates have been removed, and items that are clearly irrelevant have been discarded.

This is particularly important for projects that may have started, but, for one reason or another, have stalled. When this happens, it means the project is sitting on the back burner taking up valuable space. Some of these items or projects might be dead but have turned into zombie priorities—their hearts have stopped beating, but their body is still lumbering around with arms outstretched. They are lurking in the shadows, waiting to take hold of you (and your limited attention). You never know if or when they might catch up with you.

Backlog items related to stealth or rogue projects are another tricky topic. These items include priorities, typically in larger organizations, related to work that leaders are unaware of, whether the efforts were hidden intentionally for some reason or just happen to be playing out of sight. My advice is to be careful.

Realize that at some point, these hidden priorities will inevitably be exposed. If they're that important and seem like they're ready to be called up to the big leagues (i.e., moved onto your list of active priorities), it's probably time for a candid discussion with stakeholders—especially those who don't yet know they're one. Much like keeping two sets of books for accounting

---

6. Dr. Henry Cloud, *Necessary Endings: The Employees, Businesses, and Relationships That All of Us Have to Give Up in Order to Move Forward*, read by Henry Cloud (Harper Audio; 2011), Audible audiobook, unabr., 7 hrs., 15 min.

purposes (or romantic partners), keeping two sets of backlogs or priority lists can quickly get you into trouble.

The main benefit of having a backlog is how easy it makes toggling between the right priorities as circumstances change. With a healthy, well-pruned backlog in place, you should be able to pull items off and into your list of active priorities, and vice-versa, with minimal friction.

That said, maintaining a prioritized backlog is a key challenge that teams face. If it's not clear from previous discussions, this task shouldn't be taken for granted. As you surely know, it can be hard enough to find the time to prioritize your current priorities, much less items sitting in your backlog. It's doubly so when a larger team is involved. In fact, when prioritizing with a large team, you'll probably have to be even more vigilant in maintaining and ensuring that appropriate team members are truly taking ownership of their items and priorities. It's all too easy for backlogs to fall victim to the tragedy of the commons—for them to become somebody else's problem.

Even once everyone agrees to take part in prioritization and backlogging, you're not necessarily out of the woods. No doubt some will push back on your tools and techniques. In my experience, if you're using tools such as Simple Weighted Scoring to manage your backlog, about half the people you show your backlog to may have some angst about it because they don't want a computer to tell them what to do. In these kinds of situations, remember to explain that Simple Weighted Scoring is just a way to guide decisions, not make them for you. It's simply a tool that helps express why your decision options are the way they are. However, you move ahead, be transparent with your team and yourself about why you're doing what you do.

As I learned the hard way at Virtual Vineyards, the more transparent people are at each phase of the prioritization process, the better off you and your partners will be.

12

Organizational Priorities

Executive pet projects. New initiatives that put the organization into overdrive. Critical improvements that are never completed. Complicated spreadsheets that spit out new priorities like candy. What gives? When it comes to setting priorities at scale within companies and organizations, the process is all too often a mystery.

If you are confused about how setting priorities at scale works or should work, there are probably good reasons for this. First, your role, function, and level of responsibility affect your understanding of the process, as befuddling as it may be. Second, because the act of prioritizing and the process of planning are tightly coupled, if you're not sure how planning gets done, there's a good chance you're going to be kept in the dark about prioritizing, too. And lastly, every organization does priority-setting completely differently.

Let's walk through these issues one by one.

As you may be all too aware, rarely does any one person in an organization have a sense of the "whole animal" that is the prioritization/planning process. Consider the famous parable of the blind people and the elephant.

> Six people who have never seen nor heard of an elephant enter a dark room. They each touch the elephant hidden inside the dark room to learn about it. Each person feels only one part of the elephant: just the tail, or the trunk, for example. Each one forms a true, accurate, and very limited idea of what an elephant is. The person who felt the trunk believes an elephant is like a hose. The person who felt the side thinks it is like a wall.

> Each person, having never come across an elephant before, describes it based on their personal encounter with a distinctly different part of the elephant's body. None of the individuals has sufficient experience, context, or understanding to accurately describe what they are encountering.[1]

The same is true for prioritization at scale. Without enough "light" aka context, or really any transparent information at all, you don't stand a chance of understanding the beast in front of you. Plus, the further away you are from the C-suite, the more vague and disembodied the process will inevitably feel. By the time some priority-related directive filters down to you, it may seem like it came from the red planet, Mars. In a large organization or company, it's not uncommon for people to have absolutely no practical knowledge of, or understanding about, a new organizational process and its implications.

Next, separating prioritizing from organizational planning is all but impossible; they mesh like gears and are inextricably linked. Think of priorities as the inputs to planning. This means that any changes in priorities must reflect changes in plans and vice-versa.

And finally, there is no one right way to prioritize. What influences the process most is how collaborative your organization's executive leadership happens to be. Some leaders approach prioritizing transparently, aiming to co-create and refine priorities with staff until everybody knows about them and is (mostly) onboard. Others, not so much.

---

1. J. Elise Keith, *Where the Action Is: The Meetings That Make or Break Your Organization*, read by J. Elise Keith (Portland: Second Rise, 2019), Audible audiobook, unabr., 12 hrs. 27 mins.

There are other, secondary factors that influence the process as well: the sector (public or private) or industry the company is in as well as its organizational complexity. Then there are company-specific differences in the methods, frameworks, sorting techniques, simulations, software, and document artifacts used in the prioritization process. (Though it's worth mentioning that the method is not as important as buy-in to the prioritization process itself. Frankly, it matters less what the process is than the fact that there is a process that is reasonably straightforward and transparent.)

The good news—if you can call it that—is that in my experience, the process of prioritizing gets more interesting as teams engage with other teams, especially when time is short, and the stakes are high. This is a natural byproduct of an increasing number of stakeholders and diversity of potentially conflicting priorities. Under these circumstances, the line that separates episodic and periodic prioritization can start to get blurry. Be that as it may, having a tried-and-true process for prioritizing under these conditions will put you in a better position for managing, and hopefully overcoming, whatever obstacles get thrown in your path. And there will be many. Guaranteed.

On that note, I'll discuss another real-life prioritization tale, one where you'll learn about strategies like the Priorities Discovery Sprint, a technique for the Gather phase in DEGAP, and a framework for the prioritizing phase of DEGAP called the *Max Priorities Pyramid*, which I originally used successfully at Rackspace to realign the priorities in the product business unit after the new CEO changed the company's strategic direction.

As a side note, the successful realignment of the product business unit's priorities at Rackspace provided desperately needed focus and stability across the entire company. By providing clarity about what was most (and least) important, we were able to minimize organizational disruption, prevent the regrettable loss of key managers and talent, and enable operational leaders, their teams, and the individual contributors and front-line managers on those teams to get back to work.

Whatever your situation happens to be, you can draw on the principles, tools, and techniques described in this chapter to help your whole organization figure out what its priorities are or should be and how to apply them at scale.

One Company's Challenge

When I rejoined AllClear ID in 2016 after a 10-year hiatus, at first I didn't understand just how complicated their situation had become. You may recall from Chapter 10 that since I'd originally left the company, AllClear ID had established an industry-leading reputation for its innovative identity protection products, award-winning customer service, and successful deployment at very large scale.

However, while from a customer perspective the company's software platform was rock solid, stable, and secure, internally things were a lot more complicated. The software was difficult to maintain and finicky to update, which unsurprisingly led to a lot of stress among employees. Given the nature of AllClear ID's business, it was not possible to schedule even a moment of downtime for maintenance. The platform had to stay up and running day and night, 24 hours a day, seven days a week, every day of the year. Additionally, developing and deploying new features and capabilities was very difficult because of how interdependent and tightly coupled all of the system's features and functions were. If you tried to improve something, there was a good chance it would have unforeseen consequences downstream.

As the newly hired VP of Product, my objective was to figure out how to alleviate the crushing pressure the business was under and to scale up its people, capabilities, core processes, and technology platform. My role, which at first seemed exciting, now looked daunting. Little did I realize before accepting the job how critical my understanding of prioritization would turn out to be. At the time, though, I didn't really know it.

The company was staring down a dizzying array of conflicting imperatives. In large part, this stemmed from their dire need to modernize their software platform, which had been stretched to the breaking point. They also needed to rebuild the teams, processes, data governance, and other operational technology required to support existing clients as well as new ones. Meanwhile, an unrelenting storm of data breaches targeting our customers, among them Sony, Home Depot, and other global brands, loomed in the background.

What to fix, who to hire, what features to build, which processes to automate? What to do now, later…maybe never? I had no clue where to start.

It quickly became obvious that the best path forward—truthfully, my only path—was to leverage DEGAP to gain deep insight into our current state, our desired state, and what would need attention, time, and resources to close the gap between them. The stakes were high, and the situation warranted a methodical approach. At least time was on my side. Or so I thought.

The Priorities Discovery Sprint

I desperately needed a way to unearth the reality of the present situation—to pinpoint solutions to problems, highlight opportunities, seek insight into existing priorities (both tacit and explicit), and determine what priorities should actually be in play. In other words, it was time to embark on a Priorities Discovery Sprint, a structured approach for the Gather phase of DEGAP.

An approach to due diligence that was derived from the Agile software development methodology, the Priorities Discovery Sprint is perhaps best thought of as a timeboxed investigation for gaining awareness of and gathering intelligence about complex situations.[2] *Priorities Discovery* refers to the task of identifying individual items (potential priorities) and information about them; the *Sprint* is about doing this quickly. The intent of the sprint is to orient your team to your current as-is state, determine your desired to-be state, and then figure out what needs to be prioritized to close the gap.

Naming such an investigation *Discovery* has the benefit of putting a friendly label on what might seem like a scary diagnostic process. It helps legitimize what some people might fear is (or could become) a blame game, even though nothing could be further from the truth, especially if the process is handled as an objective fact-finding mission. It gives you, the lead detective, psychological permission to gather complaints, symptoms, and causes, as well as more aspirational goals and objectives (or OKRs—objectives and key results). By separating diagnosing from solutioning, the Priorities Discovery Sprint aims to *identify* and *gain* insight into items, not to *solve* for what comes up. This is a very important point.

The sprint is accomplished by talking with stakeholders, which is part of gathering information (in DEGAP). In this case, the term refers to subject matter experts, leaders, veteran front-line employees, and others who know

---

2. Note that proponents of Agile software development typically use the concept of a "sprint" as a method for performing and completing work in a timebox.

what's going on—the people who "know where the bodies are buried," so to speak. Bonus points if they know *why* they're buried, e.g., how the organization's strategy and execution got off track.

A Priorities Discovery Sprint is especially useful in larger organizations where complex problems or vague opportunities are nearly impossible for any one person to fully grasp—to see the big picture and know what it means practically. People in various functions and at different levels of the organization, much like the blind people describing the elephant, see things from their own unique vantage point. Senior leaders' perspectives are shaped by information that's typically not available to people on the front lines; managers and individual contributors, on the other hand, draw from a more realistic understanding of what's happening in day-to-day operations.

It's this very disconnect within the hierarchy that contributes to a lack of mutual understanding when it comes to organizational priorities. No one knows or can explain how lower-level priorities and activities should link up to higher-level objectives and workstreams. The disconnect can be especially harmful in times of increased uncertainty when leaders feel compelled to make decisions without enough high-value information out of a fear of being indecisive.

A Priorities Discovery Sprint is also beneficial to large organizations when nobody has the political power or organizational clout to convene stakeholders in a structured multiday event geared toward eliciting candid feedback, like a Future Search Conference.[3]

How the Priorities Discovery Sprint Works

At its core, the Priorities Discovery Sprint process involves identifying and interviewing stakeholders, understanding the problem space or opportunity domain, figuring out how to judge what is most versus least important, identifying and ranking items (potential priorities), and then reporting or presenting the findings. Once this is done, you and your team will be in a far stronger position to determine what to do next.

---

3. Merrelyn Emery and Ronald Purser, *The Search Conference: A Powerful Method for Planning Organizational Change and Community Action* (Hoboken, NJ: Jossey-Bass, 1996).

In my experience, a sprint can range from two to six weeks, depending on the complexity of the organization and the challenges that it faces. At a minimum, a sprint should have a directly responsible individual or "DRI" as they like to call them at Apple. More commonly, however, a small cross-functional team is responsible for the investigation and diagnosis that ultimately gets revealed and presented at the end of the sprint.

The next tasks for this person or team include the following:

1. Define the purpose and scope of the discovery effort.

2. Frame the problem or opportunity by clarifying outcome drivers.

3. Get feedback from stakeholders (fact-finding).

4. Interpret the results.

5. Report the findings to decision-makers and stakeholders.

You can declare your Priorities Discovery Sprint successful when the majority of stakeholders agree that the organization's North Star—the one priority, goal, metric, or mission that every other, subsidiary priority should point toward—has been identified, other high-level items/priorities have been proposed, and the categories and completion time horizons of those priorities are clear.

Sprint Toward Your Pyramid

New managers and leaders typically have a short honeymoon period before they get completely caught up in the day-to-day problems and intrigues of their new role. So, when I started my job at AllClear ID, I wanted to exploit this short-lived freedom to learn everything I could as quickly as possible. This meant taking it upon myself to kick off a Priorities Discovery Sprint. Jamie May, the former Vice President of Operations at AllClear ID, once told me that when it comes to initiatives like this, "Taking the lead gives you the authority; having the title helps." So true.

As soon as I started back at AllClear ID, I observed that team members were showing signs of fatigue and burnout. And, having been informed that the team had been running at full tilt for some time, I suspected they didn't have much additional patience for what might have appeared to be a new leader's pet bureaucratic process—a lot of talk and no immediate action. I'd have to tread carefully if I was going to make this work.

Preparation

To increase the chances that a sprint would get off the ground successfully, I determined there were six things I needed to do to prepare:

1. **Set expectations with stakeholders.** I didn't want to surprise anybody. I felt it was essential to give them a heads-up on what I intended to do. So, I informed them that I was about to run a process to identify the whole organization's top priorities.

2. **Make a reasonable, educated guess about what the output of my efforts would look like.** In my experience this is a proven best practice for investigating just about anything, and especially so if you're about to embark on a Priorities Discovery Sprint. When I wrap up, what will the deliverables, report, or presentation look like? In anticipation, I developed a sprint-related template for a PowerPoint-style presentation.

3. **Prepare and publicly display my framework in advance.** In the interest of full transparency, I felt it was important to show my work publicly. I chose to sketch out my Max Priorities Pyramid (discussed next) on a rolling whiteboard. It seemed like the best option at the time, largely because we were all in the office together. Moreover, it allowed me to work on a very large, physical surface with Post-it notes and colored pens. Alternatively, I could have started by printing a poster-sized version or using a collaborative online white boarding app.

4. **Jot down a set of questions that jumpstart the conversations I want to have.** Crucially, these were informed by what I already knew about the challenges and opportunities facing the company at the time. A couple of examples included: What's working well? What do you see as a challenge?

5. **What would you fix if I gave you a magic wand?** And so on. The key is to come up with open-ended questions that spur the interviewee to provide subjective answers. Leading or yes-no questions will rarely give you the kind of intel you're looking for.

6. **Write down example items and display them.** I did this before I even started meeting with anybody. I generated and wrote down dozens of potential items on 3x3 Post-it notes and stuck them onto the rolling whiteboard. Starting with a blank sheet of paper is awkward. It's far easier for people to react to something than to create it from scratch.

So, offer up a few items (potential priorities), possible buckets in which those items could reside, and even some initial criteria for evaluating the items against each other.

When it comes time to talk, feel free to start anywhere on the list of items. Just be sure to start somewhere. Get those priorities out of your head, and especially theirs! This is really important when you're dealing with a complex situation and time is pressing. In circumstances like this, it's best just to start sticking items up on the wall without thinking too much. You can rearrange them once they're out of your head and you can see them. But do your stakeholders a huge favor by giving them something to see and react to. Everyone will be better off for it.

After everyone's priorities have been established and agreed upon, however, you're not yet in the clear. Chances are you'll still need a way to leverage the priorities of multiple team members if you want to achieve your highest-level objectives—and, ideally, do so in a way that helps you navigate potentially conflicting priorities among individuals. One way to do this is with a purpose-built pyramid to illustrate important relationships among priorities.

Introducing the Max Priorities Pyramid

The Max Priorities Pyramid is a general-purpose framework for illustrating the relationship among items that span across time and categories. Think of it as a visual canvas. It's not application- or domain-specific in the way, say, the Kano model applies to product/service design, or the Hanlon method works for healthcare. Where the Max Priorities Pyramid shines is in its flexibility across industry and disciplines.

The Max Priorities Pyramid relies on Stack Ranking to fill out a pyramid structure. Its unique design makes it easy to capture, organize, and then see critical relationships among multiple competing priorities that may not be self-evident if they were organized in conventional categories—organizational functions like sales, marketing, product development, operations, etc.

The pyramid structure highlights important differences between items that are urgent and tactical versus important and strategic, allows for useful but arbitrary categories for organizing items, and supports the use of different sets of evaluation criteria at each time horizon.

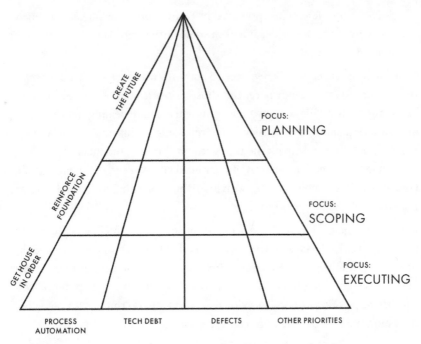

The Max Priorities Pyramid.

In the illustration example, the organizing categories at the bottom of the pyramid are Process Automation, which represents priorities related to automating manual efforts; Tech Debt, for priorities related to refactoring flimsy temporary solutions; Defects of all kinds (bugs, performance problems, usability glitches); and Other Priorities, a catch-all bucket for new features, capabilities, and enhancements. Organizing categories like these typically emerge as affinity groups—items that are related to one another in important but unconventional ways. With the help of your stakeholders, you create these categories.

Along the way, the Max Priorities Pyramid encourages dialogue, participation, and collaboration among a wide variety of stakeholders. It works well in person and translates seamlessly into a shared whiteboard space.

The pyramid's vertical axis represents time. The item or items in the top stage point toward highest-level, long-term future priorities, whereas items in the bottom stage represent near-term and now priorities. Items in the middle connect the priorities in the bottom layer to the top priority or priorities. The magic of the pyramid is how it helps to connect the items in the middle stage to fill in what author-speaker Nilofer Merchant calls the *Air Sandwich*, "the empty void in an organization between the high-level strategy conjured up in the stratosphere and the realization of that vision down on the ground."[4]

By highlighting the role of time, the framework usefully ties into an organization's strategy. It also ensures three types of alignment: directional alignment; alignment clarified via feedback loop, for execution coherence; and lateral cross-functional alignment, which helps ensure operational viability.

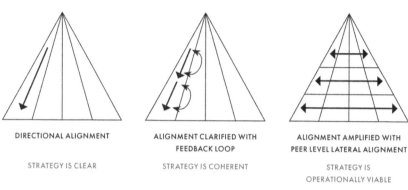

DIRECTIONAL ALIGNMENT   ALIGNMENT CLARIFIED WITH FEEDBACK LOOP   ALIGNMENT AMPLIFIED WITH PEER LEVEL LATERAL ALIGNMENT

STRATEGY IS CLEAR   STRATEGY IS COHERENT   STRATEGY IS OPERATIONALLY VIABLE

Strategy priorities alignment.

The first thing the Max Priorities Pyramid does is help stakeholders visualize directional alignment. It does this by showing the connection between the organization's North Star priority and the other priorities that link the organization's desired future with its current situational needs. Understanding this alignment (or misalignment) can dramatically improve the chances that any choices the organization makes in the heat of the moment support its long-term objectives.

Second, the pyramid helps team members conceptualize a feedback loop that connects near-term priorities to longer-term ones. This helps teams operationalize their priorities by making sure that as capacity frees up, any items that move into the foreground are drawn from a list of options that connect back to the North Star.

And finally, the pyramid ensures that the organization's strategy is operationally viable, because the alignment is amplified by lateral, peer-level relationships across similar time horizons.

4. Nilofer Merchant, *The New How* (Sebastopol, CA: O'Reilly, 2014).

Quick note: While the Max Priorities Pyramid will help teams identify, categorize, and rank potential items—that is, find the right priorities—it may not be the best tool for managing and maintaining the items once they're captured. Depending on your circumstances, that job may be better left to a purpose-built tool or spreadsheet so you can employ a more quantitative approach to sorting.

That's the theory behind the Max Priorities Pyramid. As you can probably tell, it's deeply informed by the DEGAP model and incorporates its key actions. When you're ready to see how it all works in practice, here's a 10-step playbook for using it.

DEGAP for the Max Priorities Pyramid, a 10-Step Playbook

Here's an overview of the steps for completing your Max Priorities Pyramid:

Engage

Step 1: Identify stakeholders.

Gather

Step 2: Interview stakeholders.

Step 3: Establish criteria for stack-ranking items.

Step 4: Identify items (potential priorities).

Step 5: Compare items against the North Star priority.

Arrange

Step 6: Categorize other items by buckets or logical affinity.

Step 7: Separate items by broad time (or investment) horizons.

Step 8: Fill out the remainder of the Max Priorities Pyramid.

Step 9: Determine meaningful dependencies.

Prioritize

Step 10: Arrange items in order of importance.

From there, you can refine the canvas. Now let's look under the hood.

Engage

STEP 1: IDENTIFY STAKEHOLDERS.
Refer to Chapters 3 and 4 for more detailed information on how to think about and identify stakeholders.

Gather

STEP 2: INTERVIEW STAKEHOLDERS.
Interviewing stakeholders via a systematic process of gathering information such as the Priorities Discovery Sprint has several benefits. Chiefly, your confidence will help you establish an air of informality during each of your conversations. You'll be more relaxed, and this will help you establish trust and begin to build relationships with each of the people you end up interviewing. Goodness is the result.

When you start talking to people, ask them not to limit themselves to a single discussion topic (say, projects) unless you intend to expand the scope of the investigation in later conversations. Instead, probe for information on all categories of items. By doing this, you ensure that you'll hear about whatever's on the person's mind, not their thoughts on a topic they may have limited interaction or knowledge about.

When it was time to interview stakeholders at AllClear ID, my first move was to provide some very brief background about what I was doing, why it was important, and how seriously I took confidentiality. I assured the person I was talking to that I would keep the contents of our conversation completely private and that my intention was simply to understand the situation at AllClear ID whether the news was good, bad, or somewhere in between. I wanted and needed honesty. Only with this approach could I begin to pinpoint what was wrong at the company and start developing a hypothesis about what needed to be done, as well as a plan to achieve it.

I reassured them that this would probably lead to further conversations down the line. And I emphasized that the purpose of my work was far from naming and shaming, but to set everyone up for success; make their jobs and lives easier; and better position the company to service customers, pursue its goals, and establish a foundation of common understanding. If it also helped us have more fun, gain access to more resources, and shape a stronger future at the company, all the better.

If possible, begin your interviews prompting stakeholders to identify the criteria, themes, or constraints for evaluating items (potential priorities). These are the reasons that a given item would be more important than another. See if you can spell out an initial set of criteria your interview candidates would use to rank items. Sometimes this is hard. If it is, feel free to skip this task for the time being. You can always come back to it later.

STEP 3: ESTABLISH CRITERIA FOR STACK-RANKING ITEMS.

If you have your own theory as to what good criteria could be, it's best to keep those in your back pocket, perhaps disclosing them as your conversations unfold. Don't spend a ton of time trying to come up with perfect criteria before it has become clear what they really are. Just as it is in computer programming, "premature optimization is the root of all evil"[5] in prioritization. Early on, settling or insisting on certain criteria can prejudice your interviews, leading to bad data.

Instead, try to let the criteria emerge organically over the course of your discussions. This will help you eventually reverse engineer it based on what you learn: the problems, requested new features and capabilities, process improvements, and other impediments to scaling that your interview subjects bring up again and again, explicitly or implicitly. Once you have this catalog of potential criteria in hand, you can pare it down to a short list that most people can agree on. Repeating this process so many times led me to come up with a simple ranking system.

- **Ultra-high priority:** Items essential to successfully running the business as it currently exists. If we let that drop, everything else would become moot. At a technology-enabled services firm like AllClear ID, this included customer contract–driven commitments, critical bug fixes, urgent security upgrades, non-negotiable compliance-related enhancements, and other mission-critical systems improvements.

- **Normal-high priority:** Items that would hamstring the company from successfully scaling its existing business with confidence and prevent

5. Donald E. Knuth, "Structured Programming with go to Statements," *ACM Computing Surveys (CSUR)* 6, no. 4 (1974).

it from quickly innovating its business model, products, and services in the market. This included technical and business process debt and other bottlenecks that, if removed, would free up significant resources and allow for business strategy improvements.

- **Medium priority:** Items related to the long list of important-but-less-urgent business-process tweaks, like user-experience enhancements to reduce customer confusion (which generates often-unnecessary calls to customer support). At AllClear ID, for instance, one upper-medium priority involved exploring a potential acquisition opportunity, which, if it worked out, would not only support the current business but would also open up a huge new future opportunity.

- **Lower priority:** Items that are less urgent but, while not essential, still important. Items at this priority level can include the laundry list of minor software bugs, enhancements, and other improvements that might bite back later on. Any item deemed to not be critical was relegated to a backlog.

Feel free to come up with your own criteria set and ranking system. The point is to create an easy way to flag the items that your interview subjects bring up.

STEP 4: IDENTIFY ITEMS (POTENTIAL PRIORITIES).

Identifying potential priorities is the primary task at hand. However, to some extent, "…it is more important to identify the rationale for items than to identify the items themselves." This is because, "…in discovery, you're not only discovering the scope which anyone could aggregate and sort—you're discovering the implicit framing of problems by which people are already sorting. You need to help them with reframing, and not mechanically re-sorting."[6]

On day one of the Priorities Discovery Sprint at AllClear ID, I began meeting one-on-one with key technical staff in the design, development, IT, and security departments. As we spoke, in the back of my mind, I continually revisited the proposed priorities mentioned above, re-sorting them as new information came to light.

6. Used with permission by Scott Sehlhorst.

When it's your turn to interview someone and they offer items as potential priorities, prompt them to stack-rank the items they provide. If there are conflicts among items, attempt to resolve them. But, rather than push for a definitive answer, it's more important to probe your subjects for any hidden reasons why the items are more, less, or of apparently equal importance in their mind. Sometimes it's helpful to identify the criteria or rank items first; other times it's easier to reverse engineer them as items are identified and compared against one another. Use your judgment.

Whenever someone brought up multiple items in a given category, such as "risk," I would challenge them to help me force-rank the items. If they couldn't explain why they had stack-ranked an item the way they had, I would flip the order of the items and then ask them to explain in detail why one was more or less important than the other. At the end of this process, we'd have a clear picture of what the person's real priorities were.

STEP 5: COMPARE ITEMS AGAINST THE NORTH STAR PRIORITY.

Ideally, by this point, you've identified the North Star priority—the one thing that every other, subsidiary priority should point toward. If so, compare the items you've gathered thus far against it and see how they stack up. Is it still clear that your North Star priority is the most important one? Let this be a stress test.

If you haven't established a North Star by now, it's probably not too late. Ask yourself: Ultimately, what are we really trying to accomplish and why? Once this becomes clear, go ahead and run that stress test.

Arrange

STEP 6: CATEGORIZE OTHER ITEMS BY BUCKETS OR LOGICAL AFFINITY.

As you talk to more people and gather more items, you may notice certain items have a natural affinity with one another. For instance, during my discussions at AllClear ID, I noticed that many interviewees kept coming back to one of our core processes. It was complicated and, as a result, often poorly executed. It fit perfectly under the bucket of "process and automation."

Conversation by conversation, see if you can narrow down the affinity groups to, say, less than five. Give each affinity group a descriptive label, but don't worry if an item doesn't fit perfectly into any of the categories or seems to fit in multiple ones. If that happens, there are three ways to approach things. One, you can create an "other" bucket—a general bucket for items that don't fit very well into any of the others. Two, you can tag items that fit into more than one bucket. Or three, you can duplicate the items and include them in multiple buckets. If you do this, I recommend you mark them as duplicates.

Just like there's no need to establish criteria in advance, the same goes for categories. And, in fact, trying to nail those down too early can be counter-productive. Allowing affinities among items to emerge naturally is a better approach than trying to brute-force items to fit into preexisting categories or conventional organizational functions like sales, marketing, product development, operations, etc. Doing so will bias the people you're interviewing in one direction or another.

As I collected items, my stakeholders and I continued to nudge them into affinity groups. We created categories. We gave each category or bucket a name that made sense, given our circumstances. And the more I talked to people across the company, the more the categories became crisper, the criteria better defined, and the items more discrete. And toward the end of the process, there was less and less disagreement over how the overall prioritization process was starting to shape up. Slowly, but surely, the list of categories became abundantly clear:

- Process automation
- Technical debt
- Defects (of all types)
- New features and capabilities

Process automation represented priorities related to automating manual efforts; *tech debt* was the bucket for priorities related to refactoring flimsy temporary solutions; *defects* was the category for all kinds of bugs, performance problems, usability glitches, etc.; and *new features and capabilities* held the space for incremental functionality or enhancements that didn't fit into the other buckets.

STEP 7: SEPARATE ITEMS BY BROAD TIME (OR INVESTMENT) HORIZONS.

After your list of items has been narrowed, you can start to separate each item by broad time or investment horizon.[7] When I was working through this step, I found that some items, while maintaining their high-priority status, clearly didn't belong in the overarching bucket of priorities necessary to *run* the business successfully day-to-day. Rather, these items were going to be required to scale up the business. They were both essential, but in very different kinds of ways. So, it's super useful to separate items into one of the following horizontal bands of the Max Priorities Pyramid:

- **Transform the business:** Long-term items (future, aspirational, create the future, or strategic ideas) go into the top of the Max Priorities Pyramid.

- **Grow the business:** Mid-term items (later, strategic, reinforce the foundation, or-proposed *unapproved* solution investments) go into the middle of the Max Priorities Pyramid.

- **Run the business:** Immediate or near-term items (now, tactical, get your house in order, or baseline-approved solution investments) go into the base of the Max Priorities Pyramid.

I learned other useful ways to think about these three levels from Luke Hohmann, who suggests one way you consider thinking about time horizons this way: exploit (now), explore (later), and experiment (future).

STEP 8: FILL OUT THE REMAINDER OF THE MAX PRIORITIES PYRAMID.

At this point in the process, my interviews were largely over. I turned my attention to separating, sorting, deduplicating, disambiguating, and sequencing items. After this, it was time to add them to their rightful place in the Max Priorities Pyramid.

Don't worry about creating a perfect, definitive Max Priorities Pyramid with cleanly ranked items. It's far more important to be directionally correct than precise at this point. You'll have time to clean up apparent conflicts later.

---

7. Mehrdad Baghai, Stephen Coley, and David White, *The Alchemy of Growth*, ill. ed. (New York, NY: Basic Books, 2000).

STEP 9: DETERMINE MEANINGFUL DEPENDENCIES.

If there are obvious dependencies, identify them. There are any number of ways to do this. The easiest way is simply to draw a line with an arrow from the dependency to the item that's dependent on it. But, again, don't spend too much time on this. Diving deeper on dependency mapping can come later.

Prioritize

STEP 10: ARRANGE ITEMS IN ORDER OF IMPORTANCE.

When the pyramid seems to be relatively stable, and when additional conversations lead to diminishing insights, criteria, and new items, it's time to review your work. Make small adjustments to the ranking of items if you need to. What do your key stakeholders think of the pyramid? Do they agree or disagree, or are they unclear or confused about the provisional results?

Once your stakeholders come to a general agreement about the pyramid, you can refine the priorities even further by outputting the items in a given category into an application-specific model. For instance, you can take all the items from a given category (say, defects) and drop them into a framework that illustrates the reach of those defects versus the frequency of them occurring. Or, you could take items from a category (say, infrastructure) and refine them by evaluating the effort versus cost of making investments to fix or improve them.

From here, you can further refine items by estimating their relative size and complexity and any other dimensions that may be essential to gaining understanding of their value.

In the example that follows, evaluation criteria are listed on the left. Each Post-it note contained a specific item (proposed priority). And you can safely ignore the numbers and letters in each segment. They're an artifact of the process I ran at AllClear ID in 2014.

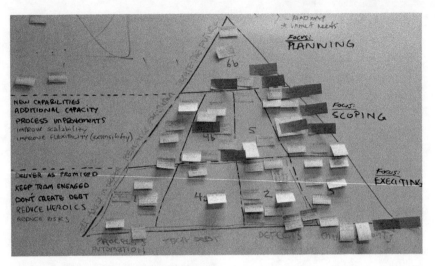

Max Priorities Pyramid from AllClear ID.

Finally, to effectively manage the items you come up with during the process of pyramid-creating, transfer them to another general-purpose tool like a spreadsheet or enterprise-class software. This will allow you to compare and contrast items by filtering, sorting, and pivoting along axes or dimensions.

Keep in mind that the result of this prioritization process is a set of options, not a directive to do or not follow through on any given apparent priority—that's where stakeholder convictions and judgment come in. What ultimately gets decided will reflect the organization's strategy, resources, and capacity to manage change over time.

In the end, AllClear ID was able to use the results of this process to drive a significant investment toward re-platforming. The board of directors released millions in funding to rebuild the engine of the AllClear ID identity protection system, putting the company in a far stronger position to deliver on its new Reserved Response offering and eventually paving the way to sell its identity protection business to Experian a few years after that.

Try to maintain a sense of humility during the process. (A sense of humor doesn't hurt, either.) The people you interview aren't antagonists—they're sources of critical intel who will teach you important things. It was crucial to me that AllClear ID employees felt like they were part of this 10-step process. In turn, this buy-in made the leadership team more comfortable with opening their wallet to address core priorities.

At AllClear ID, we were ultimately able to draw a line between the highest priorities, which we were now properly resourced for, and the remaining items that became part of our backlog. By working diligently through this 10-step process, there's no reason you shouldn't be able to do the same.

Frameworks, a Means to an End

If you use the Max Priorities Pyramid, keep in mind that this framework (like most frameworks) is a means to an end. It's not an end in and of itself. The output of a completed Max Priorities Pyramid is a set of potentially conflicting priorities. Once you understand what they are, you can evaluate them against one another using a complementary framework, sorting technique, marketplace simulation, or hybrid method. And, from there, you can use them as input to create better plans and make smarter decisions.

Ideally, the output of any prioritization effort is an ordered list with one top priority. However, the Max Priorities Pyramid produces a set of apparent, potentially conflicting, priorities that, in all probability, still need to be reconciled. This is because the pyramid produces more than one top priority. And each priority is in a distinct segment of the pyramid. These segments represent different time horizons and distinct categories such as new features and capabilities and defects, which are two of the categories described previously.

Potential conflicts can arise when the top priority in one category butts head-to-head with the top priority in another category. For example, the top priority in a category like new features and capabilities might point to the need for the development of a new feature of a product or service (in a later release). But the top priority in a category such as defects might highlight the need to fix an irritating bug in the software sooner rather than later. If the same resources will be required to address both priorities, then there's more work to be done.

In these kinds of situations, potentially conflicting priorities still need to be evaluated against one another using a complementary approach, such as Paired Comparison described in Chapter 8. In the final analysis, you still have the prerogative to make choices about what, ultimately, is most important.

And it's still up to you to figure out when priorities will need attention. Something that presents itself as a high priority in a future time horizon might require getting started on it now. Likewise, a seemingly lower priority might, in fact, be a dependency on a future high-priority item. So, good work planning will help iron out potential dependencies, sequencing, constraints, and conflicts. The scope of this book, "priorities," ends where work planning, program and project management, and development and implementation begin.

13

Accelerating Organizational Success

E ven the very best organizations struggle with prioritization—especially when it comes time for annual or strategic planning. Both types of planning require periodic prioritization at an organizational scale. However, in the whirlwind of an organization's day-to-day activities, it's easy to forget that prioritizing *intentionally* is what is essential to sustained success.

Plans vs. Priorities

You may recall our original definition of *prioritization*—the process of identifying and arranging items in order of importance. It's worth pointing out, though, that prioritization doesn't improve anything on its own. Its value lies in the information it surfaces, which informs and empowers people to create better, more robust, plans and make more informed and higher-quality decisions. And, from there, it's about increasing the chances that someone will be able to realize their desired outcomes.

Planning, in contrast, is about figuring out how to transform what matters most (i.e., top priorities) into concrete outputs (deliverables) and results that hopefully lead to desirable outcomes. Planning is about determining how an organization will line up the decisions that need to be made, the resources that need to be mobilized, and the activities that must be performed to resolve dependencies, remove bottlenecks, and deliver results to execute priorities successfully.

If you don't know your priorities, there's no real engine that is driving your planning. Because, when, "…people don't understand what the priorities are, they make stuff up," according to Lt. General Russel Honoré, commander of Joint Task Force Katrina, responsible for coordinating military relief efforts for the hurricane. In the absence of authentic priorities, people simply default to what's top of mind, most straightforward, or effortless, attending to whatever's right in front of them as it shows up, or anchoring on what the highest paid person's opinion (HIPPO) happens to be.

Think about what a typical day for you is like. Maybe you get up in the morning, have a cup of coffee, and check your messages. You tell yourself you're just going to spend a few minutes browsing through them before you move on to more important things. The next thing you know, it's the end of the day, and all you've done is respond to the never-ending incoming stream of questions, pressing needs and requests, problems big and small, and shiny new opportunities.

If you can relate to this, then you've experienced a day of reactivity. It's what losing control of the timeline feels like. It comes at you all day long, eating your precious time and sapping energy reserves until it's all gone. You never get around to what's strategically important because you spent your day focusing on one "urgent" task after another.

Strategically valuable, longer-term investments simply don't get the attention they need. Days like this end up being about "…hanging on and reacting rather than anticipating and controlling…"[1] You are fried, and your day is kaput.

Now imagine this same phenomenon unfolding in a whole organization: thousands of people across the globe—BUs (business units), divisions, teams, and individual contributors—all attempting to synchronize their efforts while their inboxes overflow nonstop with urgent messages. It's a hot mess.

Leaders and their people need to know what to focus on if they are going to be successful. They must have a firm grip on which projects, products, or efforts take precedence and which must be set aside (possibly for the time being only, but potentially for good).

People up and down the organizational hierarchy need to know which problems to solve, which opportunities to pursue, and which risks to mitigate. Without this kind of clarity, the only rational response is simply to deal with challenges as they show up. This approach is courting disaster for CEOs, top executives, and operational leaders. Leaders justify their position (and compensation) by getting results that lead to positive outcomes. It's hard to do, though, if you're flying blind.

A Hierarchy of Priorities

Another reason that organizations struggle with organizational prioritization is the fundamental nature of priorities themselves. I'll explain with an example. You're probably familiar with Eastern European nesting dolls (Матрёшка Matryoshka). For those who aren't, they are a set of hollow wood figures, each descending in size and similar in design, tucked inside one another. Each more miniature doll is revealed only when the two halves of a doll it's contained within are separated.

1. Chris Hadfield, *An Astronaut's Guide to Life on Earth: What Going to Space Taught Me About Ingenuity, Determination, and Being Prepared for Anything*, ill. ed. (New York, NY: Little, Brown and Company, 2013).

Hierarchy of priorities.

Like many Westerners, I remain fascinated with the concept of nesting dolls. I frequently use them as a metaphor to express the hierarchical relationship of a thing within a thing in a never-ending pattern. In my view, this phrase perfectly evokes the riddle of priorities at scale: small ones are hidden inside big ones, and larger ones surround smaller ones.

The great challenge with priorities for organizational planning is that priorities are simultaneously molded by the values and convictions of leaders at the top and by the imperatives held by people throughout the organization, especially those at the bottom, the workers who interface directly with the outside world.

Senior leaders have access to information typically unavailable to people at lower levels of the organization. This additional information gives them a perspective that is out of reach from those working on the front lines. But the people on the front lines see the organizational workings in action. These details give them a fine-grain operational perspective and, therefore, a more nuanced sense of what is happening day-to-day.

So, what's most important at the top of the organization informs priorities at the next level down and so forth, all the way down to the front lines, where individual contributors interface with customers, prospects, partners, suppliers, and the market in general. The same is also true in reverse: what's perceived to be most important at the bottom of the organization puts pressure on management. And management, in turn, is well advised to communicate this information to leadership.

There's a qualitative difference in information, however. Leaders' convictions about what's most important inform what the workers below them should focus on and do. On the other hand, front-line managers' and workers' clarity about the practical realities on the ground dictates what leaders must consider when barking orders.

For example, agents or CSRs (customer support reps) who talk to people struggling with products, services, websites, or apps hear first-hand about the problems people are having. As a result, reps are likely to have strong opinions on what satisfies and dissatisfies users. After all, they hear about it all day (or night).

In the for-profit arena, product designers researching market needs often have good clues about the unmet needs of existing or potential customers and, therefore, what features and capabilities need to be built to satisfy them. And IT and security staff tend to know what employees and systems need and when, based on their work helping their organization run smoothly and safely.

On the other hand, leaders have a clearer view of an organization's higher-level purpose, mission, strategy, and external threats. While they typically have a general sense of what's going on throughout the organization, their understanding is limited to what percolates up from the lower decks. So, they have strong convictions about what matters—new priorities and thoughts on how to change existing ones—even when they are missing the vast majority of crucial details.

The critical challenge for any organization involves connecting the top to the bottom—the biggest outermost nesting doll to the smallest innermost. That is, prioritizing prioritization. Some companies do this brilliantly…others, not so much.

DEGAP for Organizational Planning

In my experience, the systematic prioritization process in a larger organization often takes two to three months, end-to-end. It can take twice as long for an organization not already used to running the process. The first six-to-eight weeks are the ones most intertwined with planning.

During this first phase, managers and staff focus on identifying projects, products, problems, opportunities, and other items that will ultimately need to be prioritized. Ideally, this process begins well before the annual strategic planning and budgeting cycles for the upcoming year. Take the example of Amazon, whose planning process is described in *Working Backwards: Insights, Stories, and Secrets from Inside Amazon:*

> Amazon's planning for the calendar year begins in the summer. It's a painstaking process that requires four to eight weeks of intensive work for the managers and many staff members of every team in the company. This intensity is deliberate, because a poorly defined plan—or worse, no plan at all—can incur a much greater downstream cost.[2]

For many organizations, especially retail-oriented companies, annual planning runs through the fall and completes before the year-end holidays begin. Accordingly, management may need to adjust priorities and plans at the beginning of the year when the previous year's results and the trajectory of the business are more apparent.

If your organization has already passed the last responsible moment to begin prioritizing for annual planning this year, I strongly recommend not rushing the process. A better response is figuring out when it makes the most sense to get the ball rolling for the following year.

For the purposes of the following discussion, you'll notice that DEGAP doesn't map neatly to the four major activities required for prioritizing for organizational planning. For simplicity, however, it's probably easiest to say that D (Decide) happens when the CEO and executive leadership team formalize prioritization as a separate part of the strategic or annual planning process. The EGA (Engage, Gather, and Arrange) phases of the process are embodied in the "game" of Catchball, described in detail below. And the P (Prioritize) phase is covered in Prioritization and Plan of Record, where priorities are cataloged and communicated throughout the organization.

2. Colin Bryar and Bill Carr, *Working Backwards: Insights, Stories, and Secrets from Inside Amazon* (New York, NY: St. Martin's Press, 2021).

The four major activities for prioritizing for organizational planning are:

- **Item inventory:** Hunting down all initiatives, projects, products/services, solutions, and opportunities considered to be relevant potential priorities across the organization.

- **Catchball:** Cascading proposed priorities down and then "bouncing" them back up the organizational hierarchy.

- **Prioritization:** Evaluating what matters most, using a process that gives people involved the confidence that items will align to the organization's North Star priority, goal, or metric. This improves the odds that they will achieve their stated objectives and be completed on time and within budget.

- **Plan of record:** Communicating the finalized priorities back down the organizational hierarchy to the front lines.

Before we explore each phase, let me remind you of something important that may be obvious to some but is worth spelling out explicitly: prioritizing for organizational planning is only a part of strategic, annual, or quarterly planning. They are not one and the same. Instead, consider an organization's priorities as the inputs to those plans.

Core Tasks

- Top leadership (CEO, president, or executive director) publishes the organization's schedule for prioritization and planning.

- Leadership reiterates the organization's vision, strategy, and mission.

- Executive leadership selects an approach to determine priorities, preferably a transparent and quantitative method such as AHP (Analytical Hierarchal Process) or Participatory Budgeting (PB).[3]

- Functional and operational leaders and managers communicate to staff how the process will work and explain the benefits of prioritizing prioritization.

- The item inventory begins.

3. Participatory Budgeting "PB" is a collaborative process that enables a management team to gather items and build a consensus to allocate resources according to agreed-upon priorities.

Item Inventory

An inventory of current items of all types is essential prework. Its purpose is to identify everything that people have taken time to prioritize or put on a backlog. It doesn't matter whether people are actively working on them, planning to work on them, or investing time and energy just thinking about them. The idea is to gather a comprehensive list of whatever is consuming or might consume attention, effort, or resources. An item inventory will help you get the lay of the land. Once you have it, you'll be in a better position to match any work in progress with your organization's agreed-upon priorities.

Note: If your organization is going through this item inventory for the first time, take heed that the sooner you begin, the more time you'll have to reduce misalignment throughout your organization, ensuring that everyone is on the same page about what's most important and why. The last thing you want to do is to finalize your planning cycle only to learn that priorities are being reshuffled the day managers see their budgets and get their marching orders for the next quarter or year.

My best advice is to go slowly at first in order to be able to go fast later. In other words, take more time than would otherwise seem necessary to get comfortable with the process and the results it yields. Running the process for the first time will test your organization's mettle. It can unexpectedly stress leaders, their functions, and their people. A time buffer that gives everyone more space to figure things out can help relieve the pressure.

There are two overarching categories of items to which you'll want to pay particular attention. They are:

- Projects vs. products (and services)
- Problems and opportunities

Projects vs. Products (and Services)

Consider *projects* to be work with an end-point, often performed by temporary teams or people. On the other hand, *products* (or *services*) include ongoing work performed or deliverables created over time by teams or individual contributors who are more or less permanently assigned to a given stream of value an organization produces. And problems (or opportunities) refer to the work to be done to identify and close the gaps between actual and desired states.

The item inventory is a mandatory step when it's time for your organization to begin executing new strategic or annual plans. When priorities are finally determined, some projects, products, and proposals to address problems, improvements, and opportunities will get more resources, while others will continue as planned. Yet others will be paused or deferred until other higher priorities can progress or be canceled altogether if they are out of alignment with immediate medium-term and strategic priorities. It's essential that leaders not only drive the inventory but also take an active role in it.

Problems and Opportunities

Perhaps the most critical category of items is *problems*—as well as the flip side, *opportunities*. In organizational planning, *problem* implies any work, effort, or investment that doesn't neatly fit under the project or product (or service) label. This includes, but is not limited to, initiatives, investments, goals, OKRs (objectives and key results), risks, threats, needs, improvements, or sizable requests, aka, "asks."

The reason to prioritize proposed solutions to problems and high-value improvements is this: there's often a nasty trap when it comes to strategic or annual planning exercises. If something doesn't fit neatly into leadership's vision, mission, strategy, or top priorities, it will likely get under-resourced or ignored altogether.

As a result, when you prioritize proposed solutions to problems, mitigations to risks, or high-value improvements to the status quo, you will make a case for the relative (high) priority of responses to them, whatever form they happen to take. After all, the projects, products, and all other work that gets prioritized are, in effect, valued solutions to the gaps those problems (or opportunities) represent.

Therefore, companies and organizations will benefit from prioritizing projects and products based on the problems they solve or the opportunities they represent. Plus, it helps inform the sequence of investments and work, and it highlights what can be safely deferred into the future.

From here, the next step is for leadership to review and synthesize the findings of the item inventory. Doing so will typically yield a surprising number of projects, products, proposed investments, and other items of all shapes, sizes, and states. Once the item inventory is sufficiently complete, the organization is in a solid position to begin a "game" of Catchball.

Core Tasks

1. Top leadership communicates the organization's vision, strategy, no-fail goals, top initiatives, highest priority, or OKRs.
2. Business units (BUs), divisions, departments, and teams propose projects, products, initiatives, solutions, OKRs, etc.
3. Functional leaders or administrators provide feedback to top leadership about no-fail goals, top priorities, and critical initiatives.
4. Catchball begins. Everybody up and down the organizational hierarchy reviews leadership's intentions.

Catchball

Catchball establishes a feedback loop between executives and front-line workers that helps organizations determine what the most important is at every level. It helps ensure that all resources, investments, and work performed will be aligned and synchronized toward the organization's North Star. Catchball is key to successful organizational prioritization. Through the process, leaders, and those working below them, can reconcile higher-level priorities with lower-level ones.

Catchball is a metaphor—a term of art borrowed from Lean production and manufacturing—for passing the "ball" of priorities bidirectionally and up and down the organizational hierarchy.

From top to bottom, teams at each level determine what would need to be true to contribute successfully toward top-level priorities. Think of it as a dialog between leaders and managers and managers and their teams. It prompts people up and down the organizational hierarchy to align what they say is vital with the sometimes-harsh reality of what resources and time would be needed to address needs, interests, and goals—and ultimately achieve desired outcomes.

The process starts at the organization's top, where the CEO (Level 1) communicates the organization's strategy, no-fail goals or OKRs, vision, and highest priority to the executive committee or senior leadership team.

These leaders (Level 2) then provide direct feedback to the CEO. And this cycle continues down each level until the senior leadership's convictions about what's most important have been communicated to and vetted by operational leaders, managers, teams, key players, and individual contributors on the front lines.

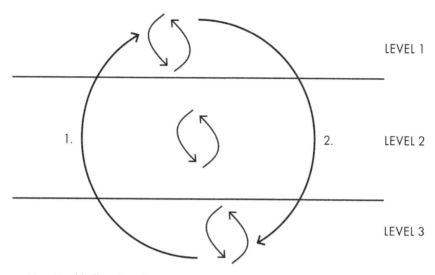

LEVEL 1

LEVEL 2

LEVEL 3

1.

2.

How Catchball is played.

Contrast this with the notion of traditional communication, in which priorities, goals, and decisions that impact the entire organization are set by senior leaders in a vacuum and then trickle down the mountain to middle management and front-line workers. When communication happens this way, it rarely matters whether the priorities, goals, and decisions make good sense to the middle managers or workers: the expectation is that they'll support the executives' decisions with few, or no questions asked.

In Catchball, leaders take the output of their initial proposed priorities and "toss" it to their direct reports in a document marked *Proposed, Draft, or Preliminary*. In passing the "ball" to their direct reports, the leaders indicate their willingness to approach the process with curiosity and healthy, collaborative debate. At this point in the process, *the ask* is to clarify, challenge, and ultimately help reconcile what they think is most important—their top priorities. In doing so, the leaders signal their willingness to achieve alignment between themselves and those working directly under them.

Once the leader and direct reports are comfortable with the proposed priorities, the direct reports, in turn, toss a draft that they've refined to *their* direct reports farther down the organizational hierarchy. Accordingly, at each level down, the details get more granular and context-dependent (for example, the CEO of, say, a chain of retirement communities probably won't have much to say about waiting room seating or amenities, but front-line support staff certainly will).

The idea is that no proposed priority starts from the top and ends in a Plan of Record without traveling down and back up the chain of command. A diversity of perspectives is the difference that makes the difference. This pattern of sharing proposed priorities helps ensure that priorities make sense to *everyone* up, down, and across the organization.

And the overall structure of cataloging agreed-upon priorities in a Plan of Record is key. It helps people embrace the plans and decisions because they feel like they've been part of the process. It's often true, even when they disagree with a given priority or decision. The truth is that people are unlikely to commit wholeheartedly to priorities they have not bought into, or ones they've not had a chance to make sense of and fit into their world.

The output of Catchball is the final list of *proposed* priorities. When Catchball is complete, leaders can engage in any final horse-trading required to satisfy competing needs, interests, or goals. Far better, they can reconvene and employ a well-regarded and proven method like AHP to ensure that priorities are fully aligned with strategy.

Core Tasks

1. Leadership, having previously agreed on the process they will use to prioritize items, review proposed priorities by business unit, division, or major functional area.

2. Functional or operational leaders in their respective areas agree on the criteria by which items will be evaluated.

3. Leadership considers items from multiple internal and external perspectives: customer, supplier, market, board/investors, other stakeholders, and community members.

4. Leaders evaluate items against previously defined and agreed-upon criteria, constraints, and gating factors.

5. Leaders employ a transparent and quantitative method like AHP to calculate difficult trade-offs, such as an item that leaders agree would be great in theory but has poor strategy alignment in practice.

6. Leaders place particular emphasis on deliverables, outputs, and results that align with the strategy and have the biggest bang for the buck.

7. Leaders agree or disagree and commit to final priorities.

Prioritization with AHP, the Analytic Hierarchy Process

If an organization is serious about prioritization, AHP is perhaps the single best approach for sufficiently complex efforts. I've waited to discuss it until now because it's not for individuals or small teams. It's more appropriate for larger organizations. And it's not for the faint of heart. Moreover, if you have a purely financial portfolio; a straightforward backlog of products, services, or IT projects; or an organization that fits into one moderately sized room, then AHP is probably not the best choice.

AHP is a hybrid method that combines a sorting technique (Paired Comparison), a visual framework (e.g., value vs. cost matrix), and sophisticated mathematics to transform potentially competing items into normalized data points for effective prioritization.

AHP does this by providing a structured approach for decomposing abstract business drivers such as "growth" or goals like "sustainability" into specific criteria. And these criteria, in turn, can then be utilized to compare items against one another. This is what the "H" in AHP stands for: the hierarchical relationships between the high-level abstractions and the lower-level specifics that speak directly to those abstractions.

By establishing an explicit connection between business drivers and the criteria required to prioritize items, AHP connects the strategy and leaders' convictions about what's most important to tactical execution. And *this* is what makes AHP ideal for annual or strategic planning.

AHP empowers leaders to collaborate by harmonizing their often-competing needs. It starts by answering the deceptively simple questions: What criteria should we use to prioritize items in contention for resources? And how should we value each of these criteria? Think of AHP as facilitating the Gather, Arrange, and Prioritize phases of DEGAP introduced earlier.

AHP is powerful and popular for a number of reasons. First, it helps resolve the tension among competing business drivers. For example, *accelerating growth* will invariably compete with *control costs*. And, similarly, *improving sustainability* will compete with *short-term profit*. But good prioritization needs to accommodate these apparently conflicting imperatives. AHP helps resolve these apparent paradoxes by ironing out the relative importance of competing goals. "The power of AHP is in being able to account for tacit/implicit mechanisms of value even when leaders cannot articulate them. By forcing the apples-to-oranges-to-wrenches comparisons, people have to develop some notion of relative value—an appreciation of the tacit value even when they cannot articulate to make it explicit."[4]

AHP accomplishes this by allowing for both objective and subjective inputs. For instance, a well-built AHP model can take into consideration financial metrics as criteria. This means there is no intrinsic conflict between ROI models and AHP. The result is that AHP's flexibility permits it to balance the needs, interests, and goals of individual leaders against the agreed-upon strategy of the organization.

Next, because AHP accommodates both objective factual data (costs, price, etc.) and subjective, tacit information (preferences, intuitions, or felt needs), it allows for variations and inconsistencies in human judgment. And this is crucial when stakeholders must end with a shared understanding but start with vastly different beliefs and assumptions about the problems and opportunities facing an organization.

The reason AHP is widely considered to be the best approach to organizational prioritization is that it nudges leaders to cooperate willingly. It manages to do this by providing robust scaffolding for leaders who have wildly different perspectives but need to work together productively. Moreover, the scaffolding is based on best practices that create guardrails which help participants agree on the specifics of the process by which they will arrange items in order of importance.

The magic of AHP is that it handles a wide range of criteria of unequal magnitude and does so gracefully. The relative importance of different criteria gets determined by assigning appropriate weights to each criterion.

The bottom line is that AHP promotes coherence by prompting leaders to cooperate willingly as they move through each step in the process. It improves the chances they will work together transparently and fairly. Pet

---

4. Used with permission by Scott Sehlhorst.

projects don't end up competing on equal ground with authentic priorities that are aligned with the strategy. And participants are less likely to challenge or sabotage results with which they disagree. The outcome of AHP is the elimination of wasteful items without politics, hostility, or the creation of "ghost projects" that consume precious resources. The significance of this improved alignment cannot be overstated.

Leaders (often justifiably) worry that formalized processes will deprive them of their prerogative to make executive decisions. But the transparency of the process and apparent fairness built into AHP helps skeptical leaders overcome any anxiety and objections they may have. And it accelerates the conversations that are necessary to get to clarity about what's most important and why.

As a result, leaders involved in a prioritization process using AHP rarely feel like they are being railroaded. So, they usually buy into the process even when the results of that process don't look like they will completely align with their original needs or wants. This is key because leaders involved in a well-run AHP prioritization exercise generally find it easier to go along with the outcome of the effort. It allows them to disagree and commit to the priorities, which is no small accomplishment.

That said, there's a major caveat when it comes to AHP. Although it's arguably the best method for prioritizing at scale today, it's too unwieldy to use without a tool that's specifically programmed to handle the higher-level mathematics. And lest you get any ideas, the underlying mathematics are simply too complicated to calculate in a spreadsheet. It's definitely one of those "don't try this at home, kids" kind of things.

In the world of prioritization, AHP is a heavy-lifting power tool. And, while it might be theoretically possible to run the process manually (in a spreadsheet), it's neither practical nor a good idea. The only sensible approach is to use purpose-built software like TransparentChoice, which is designed solely to enable the Analytic Hierarchy Process.

Moreover, using AHP successfully requires skilled facilitation to wrangle spirited conversations among participants who have divergent perspectives and competing needs. Even in the best of circumstances, it's difficult for a leader to play two roles simultaneously (facilitate discussions about priorities while simultaneously participating). But more importantly, an experienced facilitator will know how to run the software, so it doesn't hinder the process.

How AHP Works

With all of this essential background out of the way, here's a brief overview of the five steps to the Analytic Hierarchy Process, or AHP for short:

STEP 1: GATHER ITEMS.

The process begins in earnest when leaders have captured the bulk of the items to be prioritized during the G (Gather) phase in DEGAP. The output of this step produces the set of large and high impact items that resulted from Catchball.

STEP 2: MODEL THE PROBLEM/SOLUTION SPACE.

Leaders start by agreeing on item portfolio boundaries. These are the macro-level categories or buckets that determine whether a set of criteria will apply to a set of items. A bucket might be as big as a company business unit or organizational division, or more focused like a department or functional area.

Given a portfolio boundary, leaders need to agree on a short list (no more than four or five) strategic goals, top-level business drivers, or objectives against which items will ultimately be evaluated. This task begins to establish the problem/solution space.

The next piece of the AHP puzzle involves decomposing the problem/solution space into a hierarchy of impact drivers with their associated criteria and lower-level measurable criteria. As this problem/solution space breaks up into subproblems/sub-solutions, leaders begin to see the specific criteria they will end up using to evaluate big-ticket items.

The output of this step produces the necessary high-level criteria for scoring and prioritizing items. For example, what if the executive leadership team wants to prioritize infrastructure improvements? To use AHP successfully, the problem/solution space needs to get broken down into smaller problems or solutions like their aging tech platform slows new feature introductions, their lack of resilience leaves them too much at risk of existential threats, their bevy of security vulnerabilities leaves them overexposed to bad actors (or potentially failed audits), and their manual processes are error prone, costing them 10 points of margin due to allocated remediation costs.

And each of these subproblems or sub-solutions can then be further disassembled into smaller ones. One challenge, of course, is knowing when the process is starting to yield information that's too granular. That's an area with which a skilled facilitator can help. Once the problem/solution space hierarchy is identified, leaders can determine which benchmarks make sense to evaluate or score the criteria.

STEP 3: PRIORITIZE AND WEIGHT CRITERIA.

AHP employs a nuanced version of Paired Comparison, first introduced in Chapter 8, to create a matrix for weighting items against one another. Rather than a simple binary choice, Paired Comparison in AHP prompts participants to rate each choice along a range of one to nine. This involves collecting and quantifying what each leader, stakeholder, and subject matter expert thinks is important. Instead of simply choosing one criterion over another and arbitrarily assigning a weight to each criterion (the way it's done in Simple Weighted Scoring), AHP prompts participants to weight the relative importance of each criterion against the others.

For example, given three criteria for a large-scale solar power installation, leaders might want to consider three primary criteria, installation costs, future power costs, and the positive impact (social good). AHP provides each leader with the opportunity to choose which of these criteria are most important and by how much. AHP prompts people to choose how much more or less each criterion gets weighted.

1. Future Costs		vs.		2. Installation Cost
	9 8 7 6 5 4 3 2 **1**	2 3 4 5	6 7 8 9	

1. Future Costs		vs.		3. Social Good
	9	8 7 6 5 4 3 2 **1**	2 3 4 5 6 7 8 9	

2. Installation Cost		vs.		3. Social Good
	9 8 7 6 5 4 3 2 **1**	2 3 4 5 6 7 8	9	

Assigning value for criteria in AHP.

Identifying relative weights is essential because not all criteria are created equal. Different stakeholders will undoubtedly see each criterion differently, depending on their functional responsibilities, too.

For instance, a Sales VP in a consumer electronics company will tend to value new features and capabilities much higher than modernizing infrastructure.

And a CISO (chief information and security officer) in that same company will likely value infrastructure modernization far more.

So, gaining agreement about the relative importance of criteria is essential. This involves establishing a weight for each criterion relative to the others. And this is how each item will ultimately be measured. The consensus around weighted criteria are the foundation upon which everything else in AHP is built.

AHP software calculates results based on the data and assigns relative weights to the criteria so that leaders can see how the priorities are stacking up when the calculation is complete.

Weighting the criteria above results in relative criteria scores like this:

TABLE 13.1 AHP CRITERIA CALCULATED WEIGHTS

CRITERIA	CALCULATED WEIGHT
Future Costs	.35
Installation Cost	.31
Social Good	.33

Once criteria are identified and weighted, the stage is set to evaluate and score individual items under consideration. This is the point at which you assign values to each item based on the criteria. For instance, stakeholders might want to score "impact," such as value and benefits; "effort," such as cost, complexity, and resources required; and "risks," such as unintended negative consequences, the likelihood of success, and so on.

STEP 4: SCORE ITEMS.

With weighted criteria in place, the next-to-last step in AHP can happen. It involves scoring each item against the weighted criteria.

STEP 5: CALCULATE FINAL SCORES AND ENSURE CONSISTENCY.

Like Simple Weighted Scoring described in an earlier chapter, this is the step where the total scores get calculated. Also, in order to ensure that the pairwise comparisons are logically consistent, AHP software calculates a consistency ratio. If this ratio is within acceptable limits (usually below 0.10), the judgments are deemed consistent.

Leaders can now review the output of AHP to see where apparent priorities have landed in the final calculation. Keep in mind that these apparent priorities, especially in the context of AHP, are nothing more than inputs to create better plans and make better decisions.

It's important to remember that, just like all prioritization efforts, the scores themselves do not necessarily determine the final priorities. "The output of this process is the start of the conversation, not the end" according to Scott Sehlhorst, President of Tyner Blain, Inc. The leaders—the stakeholders themselves—determine the final priorities as part of a discussion and debate.

Hopefully, ironing out the final priorities won't be contentious because those involved up to this point were invited and expected to participate fully in the process. So, the scores offer a transparent look at where items landed in the final analysis: the good, the bad, and the ugly. They are there to enable a conversation among leaders. Some of the items, which may have scored highly, will ultimately fare well. Others, however, not so much.

Again, running AHP successfully demands the use of purpose-built software. Leaders should not allow themselves to be cajoled into thinking that AHP can be run properly using a spreadsheet. The software provides a structured workflow and an interface for people who are participating in the process to visualize the details, which makes effective collaboration possible.

Keep in mind that the mathematics under the hood is nontrivial. The software automatically performs internal data consistency checks and balances to ensure that results make sense. Plus, purpose-built software is designed to work at scale. Spreadsheets get unwieldy with more than five to ten items. As a result, it's difficult, if not impossible, to get the same kinds of results using even the most sophisticated spreadsheet.

Core Tasks

1. CEO or Executive Director documents the finalized priorities.
2. The senior leadership team or executive committee share top priorities to cascade them throughout the organization.
3. Operational leaders reconcile existing strategies and plans with new priorities.

Plan of Record

The last phase in prioritizing for organizational planning involves deploying the finalized priorities into the organization. Once the finalized priorities have been ratified and memorialized in some way, the senior leader (CEO, President, Executive Director, etc.) shares the top-level priorities, emphasizing the reasons behind them, the desired outcomes as a result of them, and the timeline or true sense of urgency associated with them.

Some organizations do this via a Plan of Record, a formal document or executive presentation that declares, at a given moment in time, what's most important to the organization, why it's so important, and the specific priorities that leadership has agreed to focus on.

Contents of a Plan of Record can take many forms, but typically include a capsule summary of the leader's vision, the current mission, the core strategy, company values, and top priorities for the entire organization, as well as the top priorities for each business unit, division, and functional area.

The executive committee or senior leadership team cascades the Plan of Record throughout the organization, explaining how the deliverables, outputs, and results align with the strategy and help the organization by reducing wasteful efforts.

The Plan of Record is a living document. It evolves over time. As new priorities show up, as they inevitably do, the Plan of Record helps people understand how they fit into the scheme of things. This is because there's already a methodology and framework to score and insert new items. Moreover, the criteria that leaders used in each AHP model can be refreshed to accommodate impactful changes in the organization's business or the world at large. So, the use of AHP and a Plan of Record in concert give leaders a dynamic scoring solution that makes it a lot easier to respond to new, unexpected high priorities helping decision-makers come to grips with what priorities they would need to defer or stop altogether.

This is why a Plan of Record is such an effective mechanism for establishing a consensual reality. It helps people get oriented. And it shines a light on what's most important so they can see far enough into the future that they can anticipate and control things instead of forcing them to hang on and react to events as they unfold. It helps people stay in control of the timeline.

The leader must present the finalized list of the organization's priorities as publicly as the organization's culture and confidentiality allows, ideally highlighting the priorities at the top and bottom of the list visually and publicly. Sharing priorities publicly makes it easier for managers and teams to figure out how to adjust and respond.

The value of having leaders take the lead in communicating how the prioritization process is run, what the priorities are, and the rationale behind each one cannot be overstated. Neither can their decision to remain open-minded and not defensive to questions and feedback from others. Otherwise, how else will teams and individual contributors weed out any remaining ambiguity or erroneous assumptions?

Sometimes, this is easy. Other times, not so much. It's challenging and frustrating, especially if a team must stop working on a project, product, or problem they were looking forward to solving. We've all been there.

It's also the leader's job to explain how resources will be allocated. One of the essential aspects of prioritization is understanding the relationship between relative priorities and available money and other resources necessary to pursue those priorities, all of which should be spelled out in the plan of record.

Each leader's direct reports, as well as managers and individual contributors alike, can benefit from having access to the Plan of Record. The same goes for the list of priorities, including details such as the themes, criteria, constraints, logical owner, dependencies, and other relevant data that make it possible to compare items against each other. All this information gives managers the most critical information they need to create better plans and make smarter decisions in the face of unrelenting change.

Leaders reconcile the Plan of Record with the end-of-year reality and the direction of the business, and they communicate that past this point, any changes to the Plan of Record require top executive approval.

Not that you don't already know this, but having clearly defined strategic priorities and solutions aligned with those priorities is the foundation upon which success (or failure) rests. As always, the benefits of each will compound over time. Each gain builds on the next!

Conclusion: Or...How to Finally Own Your Timeline

If you've made it this far, congratulations are in order. By completing this book, you've proven that you're ready to flex your prioritizing muscles.

When it comes to strategies that will help you get ahead, few are as useful as taking the time to catch your breath, assess where things currently stand, and then take deliberate action. In doing so, you will be well on your way to becoming a more effective manager, employee, and frankly, person. You'll probably also be a lot less stressed.

Keep in mind, though, that this book is just the beginning of your journey. As important as it is to absorb the concepts introduced here, there's no substitute for getting down to business. Without a concrete commitment to the process of prioritization—to blocking out time for it—it's all too easy to stall out, even when only a relatively small effort is needed. "Who has the time?" we may eventually find ourselves asking, after yet another trying day. After all, there are expenses to pay, fires to put out, projects to manage, employees to lead, kids to pacify, and a whole lot of other life stuff. There's always one more thing to do. Or 10 more things.

There's an irony here. Feeling completely overwhelmed, as if we're immobilized by unending obligations, is as sure a sign as any that we've lost control of the timeline. That we haven't stopped to consider what really matters. That we'd benefit a whole lot from, well, prioritizing.

Part of this reluctance may be psychological. The prospect of doing "one more thing" may feel exhausting. I hear you loud and clear. Remember, though, that prioritizing can be as complicated or as simple as you'd like. The beauty of the DEGAP process is that it's endlessly customizable according to your needs. In the end, priorities are simply just inputs to your plans and decisions. They suggest what to focus on and what to ignore.

I'm willing to bet there's plenty of stuff you *could* or *should* ignore—just as there are critical tasks you've let fall by the wayside. Wouldn't you love to know what they are?

DEGAP for Better Living

It's not an accident that DEGAP evokes two different meanings. On one hand, it's an easy-to-remember acronym reminding us of the steps in the formal prioritization process:

- **Decide** to prioritize prioritization (or not).
- **Engage** in the process with commitment.
- **Gather** items to be prioritized.
- **Arrange** the items and information you've gathered.
- **Prioritize** using frameworks, sorting techniques, etc.

On the other hand, the verb "degap" means to close a gap, i.e., to launch you over the chasm between your current state and your desired state. So DEGAP is simultaneously a technical framework *and* a philosophy. It's the letter of the law and the spirit of it.

This dual meaning has an important implication: namely, you don't always need to roll out the formal DEGAP process when you want to prioritize. In a pinch, a deliberately chosen framework or sorting technique may be enough. In doing so, you will be applying the essence of DEGAP, even if you aren't going through every step. The key word here is *deliberate*: you are taking the time to survey and select the most appropriate option to address your current needs. You are in control.

Choose what you need and nothing more. In some situations, a single framework will be enough to reveal the information you need to bridge your gap. Say, for example, you have to pick between three tasks for a project you're working on by yourself; in this case, the Eisenhower Matrix or Stack Ranking may be enough to help you decide on the most appropriate course of action. At some later point, though—maybe a few months before your annual planning meeting—you may need to cook up the full DEGAP enchilada: an organization-wide prioritization effort involving employees in multiple countries. No single method works for everybody in all situations; the unique context and needs of a situation will point you to the most useful approach(es). There are hundreds, if not thousands, of frameworks, sorting techniques, simulations, hybrid methods, and more that are being invented every day.

This adaptability is what makes the DEGAP process so useful across sectors, industries, disciplines, and roles. Over the course of my long career, I've worked in a number of industries and coached clients at a wide variety of companies, and almost everyone I've worked with has found a way to apply DEGAP to their challenges, no matter how novel they seemed.

That said, I strongly encourage anyone new to this process to start by going through the full DEGAP model step by step. Once you've explored how it works, you'll be that much more adept at finding ways to customize it to meet your current and future needs—which methods, sorting techniques, or simulations are most relevant to your own situation. The structure the process provides is consistently said to be the most valuable element of DEGAP, according to the thousands of people who have relied on it over the years.

The Future of Prioritization

So, where do you go from here?

When it comes to the future of prioritization, I would be remiss if I didn't discuss AI. Like it or not, AI and large language models (LLMs) are here to stay. The technologies that power artificial intelligence are getting more powerful and cheaper by the month. Much like computers have largely disappeared into the fabric of your daily experience, generative AI will grow and find its way into the nooks and crannies of your favorite products and services that you interact with daily.

The good news is that this is going to make prioritization a lot easier. Picture, for instance, a conversational chatbot interface that, through targeted questions, can point you toward the best approaches and tools to help you. Or automated simulations that predict responses from stakeholders under specific circumstances. Imagine a system that has an almost uncanny ability to "understand" your circumstances and diagnose your prioritization needs, and then *automagically* arrange items in order of importance superiority in rank or privilege.

Be that as it may, all the generative AI advances in the world can't diminish the importance of being intentional about prioritizing. They won't let you off the hook from engaging purposefully in the process; give you a free pass to skip gathering information from stakeholders and other resources; or let you avoid the task of arranging items, metadata, evaluation criteria, and prioritization methods. And AI certainly won't excuse you from the critical job of determining your ultimate priorities.

Generative AI lacks any intrinsic, life-affirming purpose. AI can't tell you what you know in your heart. Your unmet needs, personal interests, highest aspirations, and desired outcomes drive prioritization. Therefore, human beings will always be an essential part of the DEGAP process, even if AI can speed up or improve upon parts of it. And I say all of this even as a person who is developing an AI specifically for prioritization. I, perhaps more than anyone, sense its promise—and its limitations. Curious? Let's ask ChatGPT, an AI-driven computer program designed to respond like a person:

My final prompt: Regarding prioritization, will AI/LLMs replace human beings?

 ChatGPT

Artificial intelligence will play an increasingly important role in prioritization. However, it's unlikely to replace humans fully.

Instead, the future will likely be a collaboration: AI and humans working hand-in-hand with AI providing data-driven insights and humans contributing contextual awareness, creativity, ethical judgment, emotional intelligence, and accountability to prioritization.

AI can't recognize the significance of changes in the environment and be able to predict and adapt to these changes. It lacks the innate ability to understand context like humans do. Humans are particularly good at this because they draw from a wide range of experiences, emotions, and instincts.

This blend of AI and human expertise can create a more efficient and well-rounded approach to addressing complex challenges.

OpenAI ChatGPT's 4.0 answer.

As inputs to your plans and decisions, you must own your priorities. You can't outsource what matters most to you. It's still up to you, your team, or your organization to choose what to act on and why. Remember that DEGAP is ultimately about enabling effective action. The philosophy behind it is about empowering people. The intent is to put human beings at the center and in a stronger and better-informed place to transform what's most important into quality outputs and results. The deeper purpose is to enable more desirable outcomes and create the kind of world everyone wants to live and flourish in.

Final Thoughts

There you have it.

If you're anything like me, you can't unring the bell after reading a book like this. Like decision-making, priority setting is a skill that, when mastered, can be applied to nearly any situation. There's a good chance that at this point you're starting to see everything around you as an opportunity to prioritize or a problem to be solved. You'll never cook without this missing ingredient again.

Before I send you off into the world to prioritize your way to success, here are four essential takeaways to think about:

- **For individuals:** Anyone, no matter what their current needs are, can benefit enormously from doing the Morning Boot Routine every day. Doing it may even change your life—yes, really. The twenty-five minutes or less it takes each morning will help you pinpoint what you're avoiding, the next actionable step you must take to achieve your most important goal, and the item with the highest cost of delay. This routine will help you internalize the prioritization process, and you'll begin to apply it automatically whenever your timeline threatens to get out of hand. This is truly DEGAP in action.

- **For teams:** Your sector, industry, discipline, and job function will inevitably lead you toward certain prioritization methods over others. But there are two things to watch out for. First, just because a given prioritization method is commonly used doesn't mean it will be right in your specific circumstances; stay on the lookout for even better approaches. Second, if you get off to a rocky start, remember that you can prioritize what's holding your team back from performing its best (i.e., obstacles). If your team isn't living up to its potential, use Speedboat to figure out why. And then do something about it!

- **For organizations:** Companies and organizations gain competitive advantage through intentional prioritization. By separating the process of prioritizing from strategic and annual planning, your teams, and the individual contributors and front-line managers within them, will learn to identify items of any type that they must prioritize. This will give everyone a greater understanding of what matters most—and least. The end result is that your organization will be far more aligned.

- **For everyone:** Prioritizing prioritization is an extreme form of upstream thinking, a way of addressing problems before it's too late. And who wants to be too late? Not me. Presumably, not you.

If you'd like to further explore the ideas discussed in this book, check out www.harrymax.com for additional information, resources, and tools. And if you have any thoughts about the book, positive or negative, I would truly love to hear from you. Please feel free to contact me at harry@harrymax.com.

Here's to the right priorities.

Appendix: Prioritization Methods

Hundreds, if not thousands of frameworks, sorting techniques, simulations, and hybrid methods exist, and more are being invented daily. *Managing Priorities: How to Create Better Plans and Make Smarter Decisions* mentioned a small fraction of these methods for individuals, teams, or organizations. A brief description of each method follows in alphabetical order.

Analytic Hierarchy Process, AHP

Type of Method: Hybrid method

What It Is: A structured approach for prioritizing that utilizes Paired Comparison, a Cost vs. Value framework, and mathematical modeling to establish a hierarchy of interconnected priorities.

Why It's Important: AHP provides a systematic approach for prioritizing, enabling complex multicriteria problems and opportunities to be broken down into more easily compared parts. This method aligns well with the complexities of strategic decisions.

How It Works: AHP works by decomposing a "problem space" into a hierarchy of sub-problems that can be evaluated separately and then synthesizing the evaluations to determine an overall ranking or priority. Stakeholders compare the relative importance of various elements at each level of the hierarchy, using a scale of values, and these comparisons are then processed mathematically to derive the weights and consistency ratio, forming a cohesive solution.

Practical Application: It's particularly useful in larger organizational scenarios where multiple competing objectives need to be weighed fairly against each other.

Useful Info: This process involves complex mathematical modeling and may require a good understanding of the underlying principles to apply effectively. Use of purpose-built AHP software and expert facilitation is highly recommended.

Buy a Feature

Type of Method: Simulation

What It Is: An innovation game[1] where stakeholders are given a set amount of "money" to "purchase" features or other elements they believe are most important.

Why It's Important: Buy a feature engages stakeholders in the process of prioritizing by forcing them to make trade-offs. By forcing stakeholders to "put their money where their mouth is," it provides a direct insight into their preferences.

How It Works: Stakeholders are given a set amount of "money" to "buy" the items (features) they believe are most important. The most "purchased" items get priority.

Practical Application: It's particularly useful in product design and development environments when you want to gather stakeholder input on which features to prioritize.

Useful Info: Pricing of items is critical. Items should be reflective of the actual effort, value, or priority in order to simulate a real decision-making process. Beyond having the list of items purchased, there is considerable value in the conversations among participants. The money distributed equally among participants should amount to 40% of the total price of all the tems.

Cost of Delay

Type of Method: Framework (qualitative) or sorting technique (quantitative)

What It Is: A method to assess the cost, monetary or otherwise, of deferring attention, a decision, or action on an item.

---

1. Luke Hohmann, *Innovation Games: Creating Breakthrough Products Through Collaborative Play* (Boston, MA: Addison-Wesley Professional, 2006).

The Cost of Delay formula is:

Cost of Delay (CoD)=Value Lost Due to Delay + Cost to Restart or Rework

Why It's Important: It introduces the concept of time value to the prioritization process.

How It Works: It identifies the potential value of items over time, taking into account the potential losses if they were delayed. Use this information to prioritize items that get more "expensive" over time.

Practical Application: Use it when deciding on which tasks, projects, or work to prioritize based on potential benefits and losses over time.

Useful Info: Consider the increased cost, duration, and urgency when deciding items' priorities. Often, a quicker win for a smaller item is more valuable than waiting for a larger, longer-term item to bear fruit.

Dot Voting

Type of Method: Simulation

What It Is: A prioritization method where participants allocate a fixed number of dots or nonbinding votes to various options, with the most-voted options being ranked the highest.

Why It's Important: It provides a fast and easy way to gauge preferences and priorities, encourages collaboration, and offers a clear visual representation of the chosen priorities.

How It Works: It gives participants a set number of "dots" or votes, which they can allocate to various items under consideration. Participants place their dots on the items they believe are most important or valuable. The options with the most dots are the most important or have the highest priority.

Practical Application: Use it in brainstorming sessions, team meetings, workshops, and other decision-making processes to quickly prioritize items or to gauge the collective preference of a group.

Useful Info: The votes taken do not have to be binding. Be sure to clearly define the criteria for voting to ensure alignment with objectives. Avoid listing items that are too similar to avoid votes for an item that might be better split among two or more items. It may oversimplify complex decisions and is susceptible to groupthink.

Eisenhower Matrix

Type of Method: Framework

Alternative Name(s): Covey Matrix

What It Is: A general-purpose method for helping people determine quickly whether something needs your attention now or can tolerate a delay in attention or action.

	Not Urgent	Urgent
Important	NEXT	NOW
Unimportant	When Convenient	ASAP

Eisenhower Matrix.

Why It's Important: It draws meaningful distinctions between the urgency and importance of an item. First, it highlights those items that are truly urgent and important. Second, it highlights nonurgent and nonimportant items that can be deferred or ignored. Third, it highlights truly important priorities that often get lost in the "tyranny of the urgent."

How It Works: It categorizes tasks into four categories: urgent and important, important but not urgent, urgent but not important, and neither urgent nor important. Prioritize accordingly.

Practical Application: Use it when you need to make a quick assessment of the order you should engage the items on your list.

Useful Info: Use the Eisenhower Matrix to quickly determine if it's appropriate to run the DEGAP process or shelve it for the time being.

Fast vs. Right Framework

Type of Method: Framework

What It Is: A useful framework that aids decision-making by helping you think through how quickly you need to act versus how rigorous you need to be before acting.

Why It's Important: Understanding the context and consequences of the decision are vital. In situations where rapid response is critical, fast decisions may be prioritized, whereas in strategic, long-term scenarios, taking the time to arrive at the "right" decision may be more appropriate.

How It Works: It determines whether it's more important to deliver a result quickly or correctly. Make decisions based on this trade-off.

Practical Application: Use it when you need to negotiate with your boss about how polished a deliverable like a document or presentation needs to be.

Useful Info: Be sure that you and your team are clear about how you are defining "right" and "fast," especially when it comes to the dimension of time.

Impact/Effort Matrix

Type of Method: Framework

Alternative Name(s): Cost/Value Matrix

What It Is: A decision-making tool used to prioritize work, projects, or tasks based on the estimated value they will have and the estimated effort it will take to implement them.

Impact/Effort Matrix.

Why It's Important: It allows for more efficient allocation of resources to work, projects, or tasks that yield the highest return on investment.

How It Works: Visually plot tasks or projects on a 2x2 matrix, representing 4 categories: high impact and low effort, high impact and high effort, low impact and low effort, and low impact and high effort. Rank items in each category to one another. Prioritize accordingly.

Practical Application: Use it when you need to identify "low-hanging fruit" to tackle first.

Useful Info: Items in the high-impact, low-effort quadrant should be prioritized. Be aware that it requires subjective judgment, which may vary among team members.

Max Priorities Pyramid

Type of Method: Framework

What It Is: A method for visualizing the relationship among items that span across time and categories, utilizing Stack Ranking to fill out a pyramid structure.

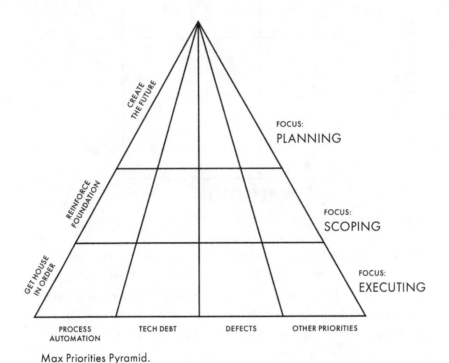

Max Priorities Pyramid.

Why It's Important: It is a powerful way to get multiple teams on the same page about what matters from high-level goals all the way down to more tactical actions. Its unique design makes it easy to capture, organize, and then see critical relationships among multiple competing priorities that might not be self-evident if they were organized in conventional categories, such as organizational functions. The pyramid structure highlights important differences between items that are urgent and tactical versus important and strategic; allows for useful but arbitrary categories for organizing items; and supports the use of different sets of evaluation criteria at each time horizon.

How It Works: The pyramid's vertical axis represents time. The item (or items) in the top stage point toward highest-level, long-term future priorities, whereas items in the bottom stage represent near-term and now priorities. Items in the middle connect the priorities in the bottom layer to the top priority or priorities.

Practical Application: It's useful for aligning operational priorities with strategic direction in a small business.

Useful Info: It can help to visualize the strategic hierarchy and align the team toward a common goal.

Paired Comparison

Type of Method: Sorting technique

Alternative Name(s): Prioritizing Grid, Pairwise Comparison

What It Is: A method in which options are compared against each other, one pair at a time.

STEP 1	STEP 2	STEP 3	STEP 4	STEP 5
Items	Comparison	Raw Score	Tie Breaker	Prioritized

STEP 1 — Items	STEP 3 — Raw Score	STEP 4 — Tie Breaker	STEP 5 — Prioritized
A. Spaghetti	A. Spaghetti 5	A. Spaghetti 5	1. Pancakes
B. Ravioli	B. Ravioli 3	B. Ravioli 3	2. Spaghetti
C. Pancakes	C. Pancakes 6	C. Pancakes 6	3. Ravioli
D. Sushi	D. Sushi 0	D. Sushi 0	4. Ice cream
E. Salmon	E. Salmon 1	E. Salmon 1	5. Choc cake
F. Ice cream	F. Ice cream 3	F. Ice cream 3	6. Salmon
G. Choc cake	G. Choc cake 3	G. Choc cake 3	7. ~~Sushi~~

STEP 2 — Comparison grid:

A	A	A	A	A	A	
B	C	D	E	F	G	
	B	B	B	B	B	
	C	D	E	F	G	
		C	C	C	C	
		D	E	F	G	
			D	D	D	
			E	F	G	
				E	E	
				F	G	
					F	
					G	

Paired Comparison.

Why It's Important: Paired Comparison simplifies difficult prioritization efforts by decomposing the process into a series of simple binary choices. This technique is helpful when the number of items is, say, less than 25 and evaluation criteria are subjective, unclear, or inconsistent. By forcing you to choose between two items at a time to determine which is most important, Paired Comparison provides a straightforward way to consolidate results to create a prioritized list.

How It Works: It compares each pair of options against each other to determine which is more important or valuable. Repeat until all pairs have been compared.

Practical Application: Use when Stack Ranking seems too simplistic and other methods are too cumbersome.

Useful Info: The number of comparisons grows exponentially with the number of items, so it will be unwieldy to sort a list over 10–15 items. Moreover, adding new items to an existing, prioritized list requires that all items must be compared against each other, one pair at a time.

Pareto Analysis

Type of Method: Sorting technique

Alternative Name(s): 80/20 Rule

What It Is: Perhaps the simplest, most universally applicable method for separating the wheat from the chaff.

Why It's Important: Pareto Analysis is a valuable approach because it helps you focus on the most significant items in a set. Although it's not a strict rule, the principle states that more often than not, roughly 20% of the causes will create approximately 80% of effects. For instance, imagine that you have a list of 10 items. Pareto Analysis suggests that out of these 10 items, two of them are likely to have the biggest impact or are most important. These items will contribute more than the other eight other items combined.

How It Works: Separate items in a set into two groups, the 20% that matter most and the remaining 80%. Focus on the 20%. Stack rank or evaluate them with Paired Comparison if appropriate. Defer further action on the remaining 80%.

Practical Application: In customer service and support, roughly 20% of the problems with a product or service are likely to cause approximately 80% of the customer complaints. By identifying and addressing the top 20% of the problems, an organization can effectively eliminate a disproportionate amount of customer dissatisfaction.

Useful Info: Pareto Analysis can be used recursively. For example, in a larger set of items, you can take the top 20% of the top 20%. Of 100 items, a recursive 2x Pareto Analysis yields four items. Lew Moorman, the former President of Rackspace, taught us to focus on work like that!

Prune the Product Tree

Type of Method: Framework

Alternative Name(s): Prune the Future

What It Is: An innovation game[2] where priorities are imagined as branches on a tree and can be cut or pruned based on their value, impact, and feasibility.

Why It's Important: It is a useful framework for getting clear about what is core and what is peripheral.

How It Works: Consider related items as branches on a tree. Cut or prune branches based on their value and impact.

Practical Application: It's used in brainstorming sessions to visualize and prioritize items, especially for product design and development.

Useful Info: This can be a fun and creative way to involve the team in strategic decisions. Encourage everyone to share their ideas without judgment.

RICE

Type of Method: Sorting technique

What It Is: A set of criteria used in product design and development that ranks items along the dimensions of reach, impact, confidence, and effort.

Why It's Important: It provides a simple, yet effective way to prioritize products and features based on four factors using Simple Weighted Scoring.

How It Works: Score items based on their reach, impact, confidence, and effort. Calculate a total RICE score for each task and prioritize accordingly.

Practical Application: It can provide an effective way to align a team on priorities when some level of data-driven decisions on what to work on next is required that ensures alignment with business goals and maximizes value delivered to customers.

Useful Info: It's important to understand that the scores are estimates and not absolute values. Regularly review and adjust scores as necessary. Note that Simple Weighted Scoring using RICE is a pseudo-quantitative method. Therefore, the results will reflect the quality of the thinking behind the math.

2. Hohmann, *Innovation Games.*

Simple Weighted Scoring

Type of Method: Sorting technique

Alternative Name(s): Grid Analysis, Pugh Matrix Analysis, Priority Matrix, Scorecard

What It Is: A method that assigns weights to different criteria and scores options against those criteria, with the total score determining the priority of each option.

Why It's Important: It provides a structured, transparent, and versatile method for prioritizing options, fostering collaboration, and aligning decisions with organizational objectives.

How It Works: It defines success, creates criteria, and assigns weights to criteria. Develop a scoring model. Fill in the scorecard and calculate results.

Practical Application: It's well-suited for straightforward planning or decision-making contexts when there are trade-offs to be made. This technique requires individuals and teams to agree on what the relative balance of these factors needs to be, knowing that the balance of these factors will affect the results of the exercise.

Useful Info: When defining the scoring criteria, it's important to involve key stakeholders to ensure alignment. Note that Simple Weighted Scoring is a pseudo-quantitative method. Therefore, the results will reflect the quality of the thinking behind the math.

Speedboat

Type of Method: Framework

Alternative Name(s): Sailboat

What It Is: An innovation game[3] used to identify factors driving or anchoring a team's progress toward its goals.

Why It's Important: It provides a visual metaphor for teams to discuss obstacles and enablers.

---

3. Hohmann, *Innovation Games.*

How It Works: It lists factors that are impeding or accelerating a team's progress. Driving factors are motive forces pushing the boat forward, anchors are holding it back, rocks are risks to be avoided, and life preservers are risk mitigations. Place the items into one of four groups. Stack rank items in each group.

Practical Application: Use it to identify obstacles and challenges that may be slowing down a project or hindering a team's progress. It's particularly valuable for gathering insights from various stakeholders, pinpointing areas for improvement, and fostering collaboration to overcome identified challenges.

Useful Info: Ensure a safe and open environment for the exercise, where participants feel comfortable sharing their thoughts. This might require setting ground rules and ensuring that all voices are heard, which can lead to more insightful and honest feedback.

Stack Ranking

Type of Method: Sorting technique

Alternative Name(s): Force Ranking

What It Is: The most basic technique to prioritize a set of items by ranking them from the most important to the least important.

Why It's Important: Anybody can do it, and it doesn't require any special tools or knowledge.

How It Works: It evaluates a set of items according to tacit or explicit criteria. Then it orders them in sequence, based on their relative value. This orderly arrangement helps to identify top and bottom priorities clearly.

Practical Application: Use it when you or your team has a set of items requiring their attention, which needs careful thought, discussion or team support for ranking in a certain order, and preferably when there is a single criterion against which they can all be evaluated.

Useful Info: Remember that this technique yields an ordered list of items, but it does not deal with the degree to which each item is more important than the items above and below it.

Weighted Smallest Job First (WSJF)

Type of Method: Sorting technique

What It Is: A sorting technique commonly used in Agile software development environments that ranks items by dividing their perceived value or Cost of Delay (CoD) by the job duration, focusing on delivering the most value in the shortest time.

Why It's Important: It quantifies economic impact and weighs it against the effort, in order to provide a clear picture of what jobs or tasks should be tackled first to deliver the most value quickly.

How It Works: It calculates the Cost of Delay for each feature or job. Estimate the job duration for each feature or job. Divide the Cost of Delay by job duration. The higher the WSJF score, the higher the priority of the job. You can handle more sophisticated applications of WSJF using a version of Simple Weighted Scoring by assigning a weight to each item based on its value or importance. Prioritize the jobs with the highest weight.

Practical Application: Use it when you're faced with competing work efforts that all seem important, and it's not clear the order in which the jobs should be done.

Useful Info: This method requires a calibrated estimation[4] of job size and value, which can be complex in practice.

---

4. Douglas W. Hubbard, *How to Measure Anything: Finding the Value of Intangibles in Business*, 3rd ed. (Hoboken, NJ: Wiley, 2014).

Index

importance, in Eisenhower Matrix, 25–28, 199

information, as kind of item, 46

information-rich products, 129

innovation game, 197, 205, 206

Innovation Games (Hohmann), 59, 61

interrupts, 94

Isaacs, Bob, 26

item inventory in organizational prioritization, 176–178

items

defined, as potential priorities, 21–22

differentiation with scales, 52–54

evaluating with criteria, constraints, and dimensions, 51–52

gathering different kinds of, 46–47

good vs. bad, 47–48

metadata for, 45–46

as potential priorities, 21–22, 45–46, 104, 161–162

Iverson, Paul, 118

J

job hunting example, 73–90

Arrange, 88–89

DEGAP process, 75–76

Gather, 76–88

Prioritize, 89–90

L

learning and development, prioritizing, 105–106

life paths, 12

listening effectively, 44–45

M

Macanufo, James, 59

managing priorities. *See* DEGAP model; organizational prioritization; personal priorities; team prioritization efforts

Max, Harry, contact info, 195

Max Priorities Pyramid, 149, 155–158

DEGAP steps, 158–167. *See also* DEGAP steps in organizational prioritization with Max Priorities Pyramid

framework as a means to an end, 167–168

organizing categories, 156, 162–163

summarized, 202–203

as useful framework, 58, 59–60, 91

May, Jamie, 153

McGregor, Eric, 137

Merchant, Nilofer, 156

meta outcome, 43

metadata for items, 45–46

Moorman, Lew, 204

Morning Boot Routine, 97–98, 194

Advanced, 104–109

Quick Start, 98–103

time-sensitive items in, 100–101, 106–107

Musk, Elon, 5

N

Neal, Clive, 134

necessary ending, 28

Acknowledgments

In any sufficiently complex creative endeavor, there are always more people involved than is self-evident. Creating a book is no different. To make sense of all the people who helped along the way, I decided to follow the advice of Shai Agassi, the Israeli entrepreneur whom I worked for as a consultant at Top Tier Software and then again at SAP. Shai once told me "The best path between two points isn't the shortest but the most meaningful." Reflecting on this insight, I decided that the best way to organize this section was to prioritize the people involved. I did this using the Navy's CEE method.

The CEE method is a straightforward sorting technique typically used for determining the relative priority of gear for a given mission. When Navy SEALs evaluate which gear they will need, they classify each piece of equipment into one of three buckets: mission-critical, mission-essential, or mission-enhancing.[1]

- **Mission-critical gear** is equipment that, if they do not have it, the mission will, in all probability, fail. Examples include boots, gun, and parachute (if jumping from an airplane).

- **Mission-essential gear** is equipment they can get away with not having but still accomplish the mission. However, it would be more difficult. Imagine the Navy SEAL's Zodiac boats—rubber raiding craft—which, ideally, have outboard motors. The SEALs could paddle, but rest assured, they would rather have the motor.

- **Mission-enhancing gear** is equipment that, whether they have it or not, has little material impact on the success of the mission. Think fancy new night vision goggles or a sexy new radio watch. The SEALs could certainly use their older night vision system and hand-held radio. But if they have the new stuff, great.

---

1. Rich Diviney, "Know Your Strengths, Your Weaknesses, and Your Attributes," *Jocko Podcast 374*, https://youtu.be/_ras9sT-CXc?si=xFNXdEML3LZIkLrd, 4 hrs. 3 min.

Hopefully, I haven't left anybody out. If I inadvertently omitted your name, please accept my sincere and humble apology for the oversight.

Mission Critical—Without the direct help and support of these people, I'm pretty sure the book would not have happened:

Frank Andrews, UCSC Emeritus Professor of Chemistry, for his guidance and unconventional advice. The late Richard N. Bolles for teaching me how to prioritize with Paired Comparison. Adam Rosen for his remarkable ability with words; Marcie Wald for her love, hyper-realistic approach, and candid feedback; Lou Rosenfeld for his partnership and uncanny ability to structure complex content; TJ Reynia for his heroic contributions; Howard Hartenbaum for creating the space to focus on the work; Mark Interrante and Mary Walker for their unwavering support and facilitating a soft landing when I returned from Austin; Luke Hohmann for paving the way and never failing to carve out time to help; Marta Justak for transmogrifying my manuscript into a real book; Scott Sehlhorst for his depth of commitment, deep review, comments, suggestions, and edits; Kate Earl for creating the curriculum for my DesignOps Summit workshop; Matthew Dicks for demystifying storytelling; Sharon Goldinger for selflessly helping me realize my vision; Jess McMullin for his friendship, support, and clarity; Rob Fitzpatrick and the entire "Help This Book" community for improving my writing process and accountability partnership; Christina Wodtke for the inspiration to follow through and proof that it's possible to lead with one's inner artist; Cathy Yardley for seeing through the confusion; and Jonathan Kirsch for sensible legal advice.

Mission Essential—Writing this book would have been far more difficult without the support of these excellent human beings and organizations:

Dennis Allison, Ward Ashman, Aspen Institute, Emina Bozek, Wes Bright, Bob Cagle, Richard Chuang, Dr. Robert Clark, Betsy Cooper, Todd Cotton, Dan Dures, Stuart Easton, Melissa Flamson, Gigi Geoffrion, Jeff Harris, Paul Henderson, Mark Hill, Bo Holland, Douglas W. Hubbard, Colleen & Bob Isaacs, Eric McGregor, Hoyt Ng, Anne Ovsepyan, Asim Razzaq, Ian Schmidt, Troy Toman, and of course, Eric Zarakov.

Mission Enhancing—Those of you listed below helped in a meaningful way, even if you're unaware of what you did to nudge this project forward. I am grateful to each and every one of you:

Jonathan Alba, Anthony Algmin, Aaron Andrew, Jorge Arango, Robert Autenrieth, Jahn Ballard, Victoria Coleman, Rebecca & Dan Davis, Steve Diller, Phil & Cathy Dixon, Franchette Dyer, Shawn Decuir, Aaron Erickson, Alam Figueroa, Mark Finnern, Brian "Fitz" Fitzgerald, Andy Freeman, Scott Gibson, Seth Godin, Shucha Grover, Verne Harnish, Brian Hartsock, Jake Haselden, Greg Herlein, Colin Jenkel, Jim Lebrecht, Peter Levy, John Long, Jeff McBrayer, Nilofer Merchant, Matthew Milan, John "Monty" Montgomery, Lew Moorman, Chris Mullendore, Moe Nath, Clive Neil, Nelson Pass, Mark Peskin, Linley Pusateri, Marc Randolf, Chris Reynia, Denice Ross, Ziad Sawalla, John Stanton, Qua Veda, Alex Velton, Roger Wall, Graham Weston, Craig Wilson, Jeff Zurschmeide, my colleagues at AllClearID, HP, HAL Computer Systems, PDI/ DreamWorks, Rackers everywhere; Virtual Vineyards (Wine.com); every one of my clients. And last but not least, Li'l Panther.

Dear Reader,

Thanks very much for purchasing this book. There's a story behind it and every product we create at Rosenfeld Media.

Since the early 1990s, I've been a User Experience consultant, conference presenter, workshop instructor, and author. (I'm probably best-known for having cowritten *Information Architecture for the Web and Beyond.*) In each of these roles, I've been frustrated by the missed opportunities to apply UX principles and practices.

I started Rosenfeld Media in 2005 with the goal of publishing books whose design and development showed that a publisher could practice what it preached. Since then, we've expanded into producing industry-leading conferences and workshops. In all cases, UX has helped us create better, more successful products—just as you would expect. From employing user research to drive the design of our books and conference programs, to working closely with our conference speakers on their talks, to caring deeply about customer service, we practice what we preach every day.

Please visit **rosenfeldmedia.com** to learn more about our **conferences**, **workshops**, **free communities**, and **other great resources** that we've made for you. And send your ideas, suggestions, and concerns my way: louis@rosenfeldmedia.com

I'd love to hear from you, and I hope you enjoy the book!

Lou Rosenfeld,
Publisher

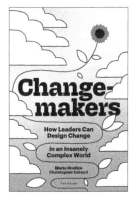

About the Author

Harry Max is an executive player-coach, consultant, and hands-on product design and development leader with vision and a solid grasp of operations. He is a managing partner at Peak Priorities, LLC.

A Silent Leader[1] at heart, Harry works with senior leaders and their teams to help them realize their visions by zeroing in on pragmatic solutions to complex challenges.

Max's experience includes having been a founder/CEO, operational leader, and strategy consultant with startups, innovators, and global brands, including Apple, Adobe, PDI/DreamWorks, Google, Hewlett-Packard, Informatica, ITHAKA, Microsoft, PayPal, productOps, Rackspace, SGI, Symantec, and Yotascale.

An early pioneer in e-commerce, Harry was a co-founder of Virtual Vineyards (Wine.com), where his designs powered the interaction model behind the first usable and secure online shopping cart.

Harry Max is an autodidact. His undergraduate studies at the University of California, Santa Cruz, focused on qualitative problem-solving and sociology. He is also an NLP Master Practitioner and a graduate of the Hoffman Institute and Aspen Institute's Tech Executive Leadership Initiative (TELI).

Harry's work has been featured internationally in the *Economist, The New York Times*, TEDx, *The Wall Street Journal*, and a Harvard Business School case study. He lives in Santa Cruz, California.

1. Jocko Willink, "Extreme Ownership Muster 018," conference, San Diego, CA, January 21–23, 2024, https://events.echelonfront.com/product/muster-018-san-diego-january-2024